Forty Years in the Struggle

The Memoirs of a Jewish Anarchist

Forty Years in the Struggle

The Memoirs of a Jewish Anarchist

By Chaim Leib Weinberg

Translated by Naomi Cohen

Edited and annotated
by Robert P. Helms

Litwin Books, LLC
Duluth, Minnesota

Published in 2008 by Litwin Books, LLC
P.O. Box 3320
Duluth, MN 55803

Translation copyright Wooden Shoe Books, 2001.

This book is printed on acid-free paper.

Library of Congress Cataloging-in-Publication Data

Weinberg, Chaim Leib, 1861-1939.
[Fertsik yor in kamf far sotsyaler bafrayung. English]
Forty years in the struggle : the memoirs of a Jewish anarchist / by Chaim Leib
Weinberg ; translated by Naomi Cohen ; edited and annotated by Robert P.
Helms.
    p. cm.
Includes bibliographical references and index.
Summary: "Memoir of Chaim Leib Weinberg, prominent member of the late 19th
and early 20th century Philadelphia Jewish anarchist community, translated from
the original Yiddish"--Provided by publisher.
ISBN 978-0-9802004-3-0 (alk. paper)
1. Anarchism--United States--History. 2. Jewish labor unions--United States--
History. 3. Weinberg, Chaim Leib, 1861-1939. 4. Jewish anarchists--United
States--History--19th century. 5. Jewish anarchists--United States--History--20th
century. 6. Jewish anarchists--United States--Biography. I. Helms, Robert P. II.
Title.
HX843.W413 2008
335'.83092--dc22
                                 2008045354

Contents

Weinberg's World: An Introduction

By Robert P. Helms

This story, told by one colorful figure among the anarchists of Philadelphia does not tell the entire story of the city's movement, nor does one man's experience with anarchism present the long and dramatic saga of the idea and its believers. The memoirs of Chaim Leib Weinberg offer an interesting sliver of a larger picture, holding to an exclusively working class, folkloric niche. The author was an incredible orator and story teller: these were the talents that set him apart from most of his contemporaries. Because he devoted half a century to practicing his oral craft, he left a clear mark on the radical culture he lived within.

The Jewish anarchists were but one of several ethnic anarchist groups that flourished in the US during Weinberg's career. Some of the other groups were the Germans, the Italians, the Spaniards, the Bohemians, Russians, and the French. English-speaking anarchists, both American and immigrant, were there in great number as well. Philadelphia had its share of each. During Weinberg's heyday, Jews accounted for the majority of Philadelphia's anarchists.

In addition to the cases Weinberg will tell you about, many anarchists of Philadelphia were leading intellectuals of the city. To cite a few examples, Voltairine de Cleyre, Weinberg's comrade, debated publicly on women's issues with the famous paleontologist Edward Drinker Cope in an anarchist club in 1893. The anarchists conveyed their ideas so well that they convinced Daniel Garrison Brinton, the pre-eminent ethnologist who explored the religions and languages of American Indians. A group of anarchist physicians, all friends of Weinberg's, founded Mount Sinai Dispensary (later Hospital) in 1899.[1] Thus not only was the caricature of the drunken, terroristic anarchist that often appeared in the mainstream press not accurate, but the true picture was often the polar opposite.[2]

Why have I, a *goy*, who can barely pick out proper names in a Yiddish text—much less read it—undertaken to edit and introduce this autobiography, which was written by a Jew, in a Jewish language, and which is mostly about Jewish people? The answer is that, if I didn't arrange for the translation and publication of this book, I would not have been able to read it, and that would have made me lose more sleep than I could spare.

My examination of these memoirs stems from my long-term research project on the early anarchists of Philadelphia, which is now near completion. Weinberg's memoirs, which he dictated as an old man to a young fellow-anarchist named Marcus Graham in 1930, are one of the few sources that shed a focused light on my subject. After it was recorded, the manuscript lingered for 22 years before Weinberg's comrades published it in book form. The book, in turn, has been forgotten by all save a handful of scholars who focus on the early Jewish labor movement. Historians of anarchism rarely refer to it, perhaps because there are so many other, more glamorous and accessible sources available. Weinberg left his mark on the common workers who heard his voice, which disappeared along with the sounds and smells of his audience. Unlike his contemporary Emma Goldman, whose amazing career has had the unfortunate side-effect of over-dominating the historical record of anarchism in the United States, Weinberg wrote no articles, edited no newspaper, served no prison term, and was shadowed by far fewer detectives. Because he gave his speeches only in Yiddish, the journalists who described his public appearances were usually writing for Yiddish papers, and so even that small body of evidence is far beyond the reach of the general public. Weinberg is a folkloric entity, and the present volume will offer the very first dose of his medicine that has been available for half a century.

The major sources that fill in the gaps of this tale include the memoirs and letters of Joseph J. Cohen, Weinberg's Philadelphia comrade; the personal letters of his other comrades, especially the celebrated Voltairine de Cleyre; the extensive published research of the late Paul Avrich, whose eloquent and thorough books serve as the desk-references of anyone writing about dead anarchists; and information gleaned from contemporary newspapers, both radical and mainstream.

These recollections are those of an old man who spoke from memory, sometimes over forty years after the events he described. He used no written records to clear the lens of time, nor did he ask others to send their recollections and thus build a more complete history. He gives a story without most of its dates, which makes it difficult to track many of the episodes for further information. I have given information for individuals mentioned as far as is available, but many names must stand as they are. I have done my best, and I hope that others will spot tales in this volume that have seen light in places where I haven't looked. Weinberg's accounts have generally squared well with other sources, and I have pointed out the few instances where there is an apparent inconsistency or a noteworthy difference of opinion. This was a man who gave thousands upon thousands of public speeches, but never, as far as anyone can tell, laid down a pen against a piece of paper. Thus we find his permanent testimony to be a snapshot of his mind, spoken on the moment, with no preparation.

There has been a need to reconstruct the picture of the old anarchist's family, associates, and contemporary figures in the anarchist movement. Weinberg has the noticeable habit of omitting from his tale everyone who did not fit into what he considered his world in 1930, *if the person had once been his comrade.* He makes no mention of any love-partner in America save Yetta, who was with him in his later life. He barely mentions the fact that he had offspring, and yet we can see that there were one or two. Also missing are his experiences as an advocate of Free Love (which he certainly was), perhaps out of respect for Yetta.

He barely mentions Emma Goldman, who was, for three quarters of the period he writes about, the most famous anarchist in America. We can easily surmise that Weinberg had never forgiven Goldman's bitter criticisms and public bull-whipping of Johann Most, from whom he drew his inspiration. In 1892, Most had treated the attempt by Alexander Berkman to kill the industrialist Henry Clay Frick with derision, which angered Goldman intensely. At the time, Most's hardcore followers shunned Goldman, and in some cases the rift remained for life. Weinberg seems to be such a case. His name never appears in the long public saga of Goldman's speeches and Free Speech fights at Philadelphia, with dozens of speakers of different radical stripes chiming in on her behalf. For her part, Goldman mentions Weinberg only once in passing as "an eloquent Yiddish agitator," in her own memoirs, *Living My Life*, which were being written at the same time as Weinberg's, and published in 1931.[3]

Perhaps Weinberg's most glaring omission is that of his longtime comrade Joseph J. Cohen, who didn't neglect to mention Weinberg when he wrote his own accounts of Jewish anarchism in America, and whose accounts included many of the same events and personalities. There was a falling out between the two at the Sunrise Colony in 1933, which Chaim never let go of. We have included Cohen's remarks in the present volume.

At the same time, Weinberg omits to criticize Samuel Gordon, his fellow Mostian, who was intensely despised within the movement for showing indifference when his former lover and benefactor Voltairine de Cleyre was near death and in need of help.[4] He makes passing mention of Thomas Hamilton Garside as a labor activist, forgetting to mention that Garside later turned up as a Deputy U.S. Marshall (see Chapter 2). This is in addition of his wholesale omission of unflattering incidents in the career of Most himself, and there were many.

Weinberg was a visionary and a passionate advocate for cooperatives. In this book he describes attempts at creating cooperative businesses, farms, and homes. While Chaim tells us the Jewish tale, there were already radicals building coops in Philadelphia when he arrived and earlier, in particular the English-born Thomas Phillips, who was friendly with the English-speaking anarchists and probably well-known to Weinberg. The present reader may be surprised by his intense interest in gathering groups of radicals together to share a living arrangement, since this is now a very common practice.

The Yiddish version of this book was edited by a committee, and they used certain editing conventions that would, if preserved here, badly distract the reader. I have intervened as little as possible, and never in such a way as to alter the meaning of a sentence even slightly. My changes have been to regularize proper names so that Ch. Weinberg, C. Weinberg, H. Weinberg, Hayim Weinberg, and Hyman Weinberg all boil down to our Chaim Weinberg for the anglophone reader. There were variations like this for many names mentioned in the book, and I have emended a few. Another change has been to reduce the number of times a word is used in close repetition, especially the word "comrade" (*genosse*). Preservationists need not be alarmed, since readers may still feel that they are being beaten over the head with this friendly term. The titles of chapters and sections of chapters have also been omitted, since they were far too numerous and not needed in such a short book. We present here an English translation of the published Yiddish memoir, and it has been necessary to do so without consulting the original manuscript that survives at the YIVO archive in New York. I don't suspect that the original had any major parts that were not included in the 1952 edition, since Marcus Graham, who recorded all this straight from Weinberg's lips, did not point out any such omissions when he made comments (included here) about the creation of the book. In the many instances where ellipses occurred in the Yiddish edition, most have been omitted by the translator. The Yiddish editorial committee may have been deleting small pieces, or they may have been using the ellipsis to indicate something other than a deletion, such as a pause or a comma. There were simply too many to leave in place, so out they went.

While Chaim Weinberg's testimony does not offer a broad and balanced overview of the anarchists of his time, it offers much information given nowhere else, and in a soulful, humorous way. It also presents a side of Philadelphia's Jewish life and social movements that has, until now, been unavailable in English. We hope that our readers will enjoy discovering this little gem of memory as much as we have enjoyed preparing it for them.

Acknowledgements

To the members of the Wooden Shoe Collective, both past and present, both living and dead, who have endorsed and funded this project—primarily by placing their trust in me—I owe the largest debt of gratitude. The Shoe has made this book happen in a few ways. It paid for the professional services of our translator, and it waited patiently for years while I assured its members that Weinberg was coming. But long before that, in 1980, it worked with Esther Dolgoff, an old anarchist gal of New York, while she hand-wrote a translation of Joseph J. Cohen's memoirs, and it hosted her as a speaker, here in Philadelphia. Were I not able to read Cohen's book, I cannot even guess whether I could have brought Weinberg's book to its present state. If that were even possible, there would have been more missing pieces than I care to think about.

Our translator, Naomi Cohen, has been essential far beyond the enormous task of translating this book. She has helped the project with her extensive knowledge of Jewish history and culture as well. This work is a joint scholarship by Naomi and myself, and I consider myself privileged to have worked with her. I wish I could, but I cannot express this thought in the language she speaks to her little children, which is, of course, Yiddish.

This project would never have been finished had it not been for the endless technical work and scholarly advice of my friend Alison M. Lewis, who is the web mistress of the Dead Anarchists web site. In my mind, there are many dead anarchists who would not have been the least bit interesting, had it not been for those who helped them get through their lives. On that note, Alison Lewis is a principle reason why this book has appeared on the public radar after its long stay in mothballs, and I am most grateful to her for that.

Special thanks go to Julie Herrada, who as curator of the Labadie Collection has turned a confusing image of dead anarchists into a clear picture of crazy anarchists.

Paul Avrich, my friend, mentor, and fellow cat lover, is the person who caused me to become interested in the early Philadelphia anarchists. We were saddened by his death in February 2006. Paul's book *An American Anarchist: The Life of Voltairine de Cleyre* alerted me to a whole world that is the subject of this book. I can no longer call him on the phone and tell him this, and so I'll just tell you, the reader: Paul, thank you for giving me this love of History. Thank you for dragging American anarchism out of the fog and into the daylight. Because your wisdom has passed through this world, this world is a much smarter place.

Harry D. Boonin's book, *The Jewish Quarter of Philadelphia,* has been helpful to me in more ways than can be appreciated with a passing mention. His book is downright beautiful, and if I should ever meet its author in person, there shall be a very warm handshake, there on the same sidewalks where both of us have been wandering.

Alexis Buss has worked in many ways, for many hours, toward the completion of this project, and I am stumped for words here. She has figured out the whole concept. She has designed pages when this was a printed book project. She has handled the material over these several years, and she has invested her wisdom. I answer with a shout of *"Thanks!"* from this old anarchist friend.

The following people helped, by offering advice, sharing knowledge, helping me to retrieve material, offering hospitality, or by doing other helpful work during the several years when I was researching Weinberg's life and the people he knew, and in so doing made this book possible: Clara Freedman Solomon, Sidney Solomon, Tom Goyens, Tony DeAnnuntis, Debbie Pentecost McNabb, Max Singer (the grandson of Max Staller), Federico Arcos, Nunzio Pernicone, Jon Thoreau Scott, Alexander Botwinik, Nancy Silberstein, the Ternisien family, Claude Guillaumaud, Pete Jordan, Shaun Slifer, Jerry Kaplan, the family of Joseph J. Cohen, Robert Davis, Jon Bekken, Robert Rush, Fernanda Perrone, Beth Lavoie, Allan Antliff, Rakhmiel Peltz of the Drexel University Judaic Studies Program, and Judy & April Rosenbloom.

The following institutions and their staffs have provided me with sources for this book that I did not find in the stacks of countless libraries:

The Labadie Collection, Special Collections Department, University of Michigan at Ann Arbor, and its curator Julie Herrada.

The Archives of Arden, Delaware and its curator Mark Taylor.

The Modern School Collection of Rutgers University and its curator Fernanda Perrone.

The Newspaper Room, Free Library of Philadelphia

The Historical Society of Wisconsin

Friends of the Ferrer Modern School

The Balch Institute and Historical Society of Pennsylvania, Philadelphia

The Special Collections Department and the Urban Archives, Temple University

International Institute of Social History, Amsterdam, Holland

The University Archives, University of Pennsylvania.

National Archives and Records Administration, Philadelphia

The Microforms Department, University of Delaware at Newark

Archives of the City of Philadelphia, Abington Township, and Montgomery County, Pennsylvania

National Yiddish Book Center, Amherst, Massachusetts

Library of the College of Physicians and Surgeons, Philadelphia

The Bund Archive, YIVO, New York City

The Special Collections Departments of University of California, Riverside, University of Florida at Gainesville, and Yale University.

The Emma Goldman Papers Project, Berkeley, California

The Archives of Thomas Jefferson Medical College, Philadelphia.

The Archives of University of Illinois Medical School, Chicago.

Bibliotèque Medem, Paris

The University Archives of Drexel University, Howard University, Columbia University, and Colgate University.

The Joseph Ishill Papers, Houghton Library, Harvard University.

Manuscripts Department, Library of Congress, Washington DC.

The Jenkins Law Library, Philadelphia.

New York Public Library, Performing Arts Division, Lincoln Center.

I also thank Scott Lamson for his help in the planning this project and for his timely reminders that I was taking quite a while in fetching out the legendary Mr. Weinberg.

-*Philadelphia, April 2007[1] See Appendix E.*

Introductory Matter from the
Original Edition and Elsewhere

From the Publishers [1952][5]

This book consists chiefly of the memoirs that the late Chaim L. Weinberg (1861-1939) related to Marcus Graham (Sh. Marcus) over a period of several weeks, which the latter had spent in the summer of 1930 in Weinberg's home in Willow Grove, not far from Philadelphia.[6] The memoirs are appearing in book form after a very long delay, but better late than never. The purpose of this work is such that its importance will not be lost with the passage of time.

The purpose, to wit, of this book is to give an idea of the substantial role which Comrade Weinberg played in the building of the Jewish labor movement in America, as well as in the pioneering experiments in cooperatives. Few people, writers and orators in the radical camp, reached in their era, the time from 1889 until 1939, such popularity among the Jewish working masses as Chaim L. Weinberg. A work which depicts, in his own words, Weinberg's life and activity, must be a very significant contribution to the history of the American-Jewish labor movement in general, and in particular to the history of the anarchist movement among the Jewish workers in America.

Therefore, we felt it was necessary to round out Weinberg's autobiographical notes with a number of reprinted memoiristic and historic-descriptive essays from writers who knew Weinberg a long time.

We hope and believe that our laborious undertaking of compiling and publishing such a work will be properly appreciated by the general reader, the comrades throughout the land, and especially in Philadelphia, the city which for years played such a great role in the movement for a cause which was near and dear to Weinberg.

Marcus Graham[7]

Excerpt from "Autobiographical Note," in *MAN! An Anthology of Anarchist Ideas, Essays, Poetry and Commentaries*, edited by M. Graham. London: Cienfuegos Press (1974).

Chaim Leib Weinberg (1861-1939) was one of the most effective orators in the Yiddish-speaking anarchist movement in the USA, and also in the trade union movement, of which he was a pioneer organizer.

In 1929, before starting out on the tour to circulate the Anthology [of Revolutionary Poetry], the Radical Library of Philadelphia invited me to write Weinberg's memoirs as he told them to me. I spent four weeks with Weinberg, and after I had written the manuscript, it was read and approved at a gathering of the Radical Library, at which Weinberg was present. But it was not until 1952 that a Chaim L.Weinberg Publication Committee was formed in Los Angeles, in cooperation with the Radical Library. The 172-page hardcover volume was published (in Yiddish) in 1952. The title read: "Chaim Leib Weinberg, forty years in the struggle for social liberation. Reminiscences of a libertarian agitator in the Yiddish-American streets. Taken down and penned by Marcus Graham (Sh. Marcus)."

On the reverse side of the title page, the same title appeared, this time in English. But the last sentence had disappeared. This was how the Los Angeles Publication Committee chose to revenge themselves for my critical position toward the *Freie Arbeiter Stimme.*

Introduction [1952]
by Thomas Eyges[8]

It is really a lofty assignment for me to write the introduction and present to the reader the interesting autobiography of our unforgettable comrade Chaim Leib Weinberg. It is also a rare opportunity to become acquainted with such an exquisite personality, as his life history brings out.

Nature did not endow him with the appeal of a handsome male: no sign of hair upon his head, somewhat foolish eyes, of which one was almost blind, a stretched-out face, lame, not to mention his baggy, shabby, cheap clothing—all this made an unfavorable impression on everyone who saw him for the first time. To compensate for it, however, nature did crown him with remarkable, extraordinary oratorical capability.

He was a man with a scanty education, almost without formal schooling, but he was well able to speak and discuss interesting and important matters and always exhibited a healthy, logical sense of the happenings of daily life.

Weinberg was an exceptional raconteur. His tales, which he used to relate in private conversations or in his public appearances, were so charming, so animatedly presented, imitating the various characters he was telling about. When I used to hear him speak, I thought he could have been a superb stage actor. He was able to hold his audience at a lecture in gasps of laughter and a minute later, become serious and solemn. Painting pictures of the impoverished, miserable life of the workers, men, women, and children, who slave in sweatshops for a starvation wage—with a rare, extraordinary ability.

From time to time, in every era of infinite time, nature produces strangely remarkable characters, people who distinguish themselves in various fields, idiosyncratic and original. Chaim Leib Weinberg was just such a type. A cigar maker by trade, with pitifully poor earnings, he dedicated his whole life to the cause of anarchism and tirelessly spread hope and striving for a free, better, humane coexistence among the Jewish working class. With a cane in one hand and a small suitcase in the other, limping, he wandered around the country to spread unity and friendship among the workers, and to organize unions through which they would be able to demand a better wage and humane treatment. To his credit, it must be noted that he organized the first Jewish bakers union, the first Jewish cigar makers union and the first cloak makers union in the country, and continually fostered this activity. The present-day big, powerful, Jewish trade unions owe a lot to the tireless activism of Chaim Leib Weinberg.[9]

But Weinberg was not satisfied only with his ideal for the future. Aside from his activity in the trade union movement, in strikes and protest meetings, he was also very interested in and devoted to building cooperatives for the union workers in general and the communal life for comrades in particular. In many cities and towns, he spread the notion of communal living as a means to ease the economic hardship of living with meager earnings. By trading in his own savings and by living together with a common dining room and kitchen and common purchasing of products in a cooperative manner, the worker could already begin to enjoy life more. But his unsuccessful attempts were the result of the fact that the participants in communal living didn't, as it were, "burn their bridges behind them." And at the slightest discomfort and difficulty at the outset of the experiment, they returned to their previous miserable life, just as the Jews, as they were fleeing Egypt, wanted to return to their bondage.

I encountered Weinberg for the first time 55 years ago in London, England. At that time, our group published the *Arbeter Fraynd* [Workers' Friend] and had open meetings every Friday evening in Sugar Loaf, Hanbury Street. Among the speakers were also Baron and Kaplan. They never agreed—always arguing. The outcome was that Baron, together with others, founded a new group, and "made Sabbath for themselves."[10] Baron sought to create a competitor for Kaplan, and at the recommendation of Banof-Mintz who was then in London, Chaim Weinberg was imported from New York for a series of lectures. When I caught sight of Weinberg, I thought, "Such a poor soul was actually brought from New York?" But when I heard him speak for the first time in Christ Church Hall, I was amazed and delighted with his humor and his dramatic movements. The words flowed from his mouth as from a spring, without artifice, without gestures, simple, clear, humorous and serious. His visit in London was a phenomenal morale booster at that time. At his final appearance in London, he spoke to an audience in a packed hall of exactly one thousand people, and almost as many were outside, who were not able to get inside the hall. The topic was: Good-bye to the Jewish workers in London. At the conclusion of his lecture, the audience really went wild. Everyone got to their feet, applauding, and screamed out "Bravo! Hurrah!" Many cried out, "Weinberg, don't leave us! Don't go away! Stay here, with us!" Never in my life have I seen such a demonstration of enthusiasm while attending a Jewish gathering. At the station, where Weinberg was supposed to board the train for Liverpool, hundreds of men and women came to see him off, and many women wiped their eyes with their handkerchiefs, waving to him when the train began to move.

As a speaker, without education, with a perfectly natural talent, I don't know of anyone who could ever surpass him. Those who heard him once in his lifetime couldn't forget him for a long time, as a 'phenomenon,' a remarkable manifestation. In my travels around America and Canada over 13 years,[11] I often met up with Weinberg at his gatherings, which used to afford me a rare pleasure from his *picante* notions and expressions.

I recall now an episode at a meeting in Detroit. He spoke there on the theme, "A World Without Money." A young man asked him a question: "Mr. Weinberg, if there weren't any money in the world, who would make inventions for free?"

Weinberg bent down to him and answered: "Is that so? One makes discoveries for money? To order? On request? Here, I will give you ten thousand dollars and by all means think up an invention. Think! Cogitate! Keep thinking! Let's see what you can come up with for such a sum."

Then he accepted other questions and answered them, and
suddenly he turned back to the first questioner, "Well? How's it
going? Did you think of anything? Discover anything? Think!
Think hard! But let me tell you that all the great, immortal
inventors were very poor, and died poor. But others, after their
deaths, manufactured their inventions and made enormously
great profits, millions of dollars. The inventor has a brilliant
idea about a certain thing, which torments him until he makes
the discovery, and nobody stands behind him with money, you
understand? But in any case, Think! Think!"

After the lecture he encountered the young man as he was
leaving and asked him: "Well, my friend, did you invent
anything yet? Something original?"

In those days, in the 90's from the previous century, there
were quite a few "idealists," who were for the most part not
true idealists. Their hearts, their souls, were full with jealousy.
They were envious of the rich man. Their envy was wrapped in
a *tallis*[12] of 'idealism' and as soon as they were able to taste a
larger and a better morsel, they were no longer "idealists" and
some of them became worse than the "bloodthirsty" capitalists.
But Weinberg lived, suffered and aspired, until the final day of
his life, a faithful fighter for free socialism, for anarchism, for
over half a century. An idealist with a noble inclination to help
build a society where every person will contribute according to
his abilities and enjoy in full measure the necessary means of
living, according to his needs—and with that 'dream,' cruel
death took him from us.

Near the end of his life, Weinberg and his friend Yetta
settled on a small plot of land, outside of Philadelphia, on a
farm, where they raised chickens and took in summer
boarders. Comrades often got together at his place[13] and
listened to Weinberg's stories, of which he was a master teller.

The future honest, nonpartisan Jewish historian, who will
write and describe the rise and development of the Jewish
radical labor movement, will surely cite, with great respect,
Chaim Leib Weinberg, among other noble types of men and
women of those times, who tirelessly labored to spread among
humanity the ideas of a free life for future generations.

Chapter 1

Well, where should I begin? Where I was born? The name of the town? The day and the year? And how I behaved as a youngster? Did I, in my childhood, already show signs of rebellion?

To all of these questions, I refuse to give an answer. Almost everyone who writes his autobiography does not fail to dwell upon all of these details. And often fabricated ones as well. Many of the experiences described will lack dates. Many will also lack names, especially the first names of the persons. This comes from the fact that I never recorded any of the important moments I experienced in my life.

Since my parents[14] were eminent land owners in our town, I was consequently a well-to-do child. When I finished the elementary school in our town, my parents wanted to send me for further education in a gymnasium.[15] But just at that time, the gymnasium burned down. One day my father said to me, "Do you know what, Chaim? I'll send you to Bialystok and there you will enter the yeshiva and study to be a rabbi."

I arrived in the big city, and right after that I came to the yeshiva. In the yeshiva, a terrible filth prevailed, such that after six months of being there I had to leave and return home. I wasn't too keen on studying for the rabbinate, anyway. During that period, my mother died. I was then 18 years old.

Right after my mother's death, I left Russia and went to London. In London I managed to struggle a great deal, like every greenhorn in our America.

The first speech, which I still remember to this day, that made a deep impression on me, was a speech on a corner of the London streets with the then-famous English atheist Bradlaugh.[16] I don't know if the Lord of the World was very angry with me for absentmindedly stopping in the street and hearing someone actually expressing a doubt in His majestic existence. But this was not my fault; He could have made it such that I, Chaim, would stop and hear a pious Jew praising His Excellence... But God and His wonders did not stop with that. Right after hearing the atheistic speech, God demonstrated a new miracle. And it just had to happen not to Rothschild, for example, but to me, that I should slip on an orange peel. And not all slipping is created equal. He, the Lord of the World, had given, it seems, a command, that the slip shouldn't be an ordinary stumble and that's the end of it. No, the slip had to be with such a powerful force that I should break my leg.

Just so did God Himself "arrange"—as if the religious folks would have liked to have provided the most "convincing" evidence to reinforce Bradlaugh's heretical ideas about God and his sentence of justice—that is, if He really exists.

I was laid up in a London hospital for six weeks with my broken foot. After that, I was sent to a convalescent home funded by Rothschild. Everything there was so beautiful and wondrous: nature in the open country, the tidiness of the rooms, and the food. However, with all of the treats, there was one additional item which negated everything. It made one forget about the bright sun in the daytime and the shining stars at night. Forget about the fresh, fragrant air, the pleasant feeling of the rooms and the food. Wherever one turned, one word was heard and became the master of the moment. And this was none other than the RULES of the place. We modern folk know what a tasty treat this is, but at that time it was a brand new thing. New or old, it didn't appeal to me. It began to suffocate and disgust me such that I didn't want to stay the four weeks that were granted me, and I left before the end of the vacation.

After leaving Rothschild's institution, I struggled for another year in London. Everything went so "well" for me that I took my bag and baggage and returned to Tshekhanovtse, Grodne Province, my birthplace.[17]

Upon my return to Russia, I immediately received an invitation to present myself for priziv (military service). The authorities had no choice but to give me a white ticket (meaning unsuitable for the military) because with one healthy foot and the other limping, one cannot run far on the battlefield.

After spending over a year in Tshekhanovste, at the age of 21 years, I left Russia for the second time. This time I didn't go to England, but to America.[18] In the "golden" land, as the greenhorns used to call America, I became a peddler. Climbing the stairs convinced me that gold has little in common with America and peddlers. Discouraged by my drudging away for a hand-to-mouth existence, I couldn't even stay here as long as I did in England. After eight or nine months of being in the Golden Land, I went back to Tshekhanovtse.

Upon my return from America, my father decided to make of me a respectable adult like anyone else. He was not satisfied with my wandering about in England and America, so he decided to marry me off as is appropriate for a bourgeois child.

The hassle of matchmaking proved to be worse than my suffering in England and America and even worse than in Rothschild's convalescent institution.

After two years of torment I left the town and traveled for the second time to America. Returning to America, I was already without those fantasies of gold lying around on the streets. I had made for myself one firm decision: to learn a trade. Soon after my arrival I went to learn cigar-making.

After three weeks of learning about cigars I spied an advertisement saying that cigarette makers are desired in Durham, North Carolina, by a Mr. Duke (later the biggest tobacco millionaire in America). The employer, A. Blum, brought me and several others from New York directly to Mr. Duke's factory in North Carolina. We were ordered to sign a contract for six months. The contract read: each week one dollar will be deducted from our wages to pay for the expense of bringing us there. There were about 200 workers in the factory. Among them were people from Bialystok, Odessa and Vilna. Ninety-five percent of the workers were Jews.[19]

In Mr. Duke's factory there were two workers who soon became known to all of us. These were two young men, Goldgar and Lieberman. They were revolutionaries while still in Russia.[20] Understandably, they felt a sort of obligation to organize the factory. And they set to work at it. They didn't, it turns out, even give a thought about a printing shop, and perhaps there wasn't such a thing in Durham.

Sitting at work one day someone slipped me a hand-printed card and directed me to read it and then pass it on to a second, the second to a third, and so on. Glancing at the card I saw in large letters that we were all called in the evening to attend a "lunch." In those days we workers were considerably underfed, so who would consider calling us to anything other than lunch, to eat?

I was lodging with a worker, Miller, who worked with us. Walking home, I said to him, "Why should we go eat supper when they're going to give us food this evening in a hall?" Miller laughed heartily and explained to me that this wouldn't be a "lunch" (*mitig*) but rather a meeting.

In the evening I went with Miller to the meeting. I had no idea what was going to take place there. My curiosity grew steadily. Finally we were in the hall, which was filled with workers.

A young man appeared on the platform and opened the meeting, introducing Goldgar as the first speaker. This was the first time I had heard a worker addressing other workers. Goldgar got more and more fired up. Warming up, he worked himself up to an emotional, fiery enthusiasm which engulfed everyone gathered there. His every word rang out like thunder. To this very day, I can still hear his passionate speech. "Mr. Duke gets richer and richer every day, and we're getting poorer. From whom does he get his wealth if not from our labor? So what should we do in order to be able to improve our situation and get more out of life? There is only one way: to organize ourselves in a powerful union. One for all and all for one!" The hall was stirring with applause after his speech.

Goldgar's abovementioned speech was, as a matter of fact, my first lesson in trade unionism. After his speech, however, everything was strangely incomprehensible, even chaotic, and I said to myself, In New York I almost starved to death. A man brought me to Mr. Duke's factory, where I'm already making nine dollars a week. A speaker comes and claims that I'm enriching Mr. Duke.

At the second meeting Goldgar called out that any of the assembled workers may ask questions. From everyone there, I was the only one who wanted to pose a question. Goldgar asked me to come up on the stage. On the way up I saw two hundred faces, each one looking at me. I immediately become frightened of them. My face became inflamed. Nowadays we have a name for this: stage fright. I spoke for a few minutes. I have never been able to remember not only whether I asked any sort of question, or what the question was, I can't even recall what I said in those few minutes. All that remains in my memory is: at the end of my speech I heard people clapping and shouting "Bravo!" I remember that I asked Goldgar what people were applauding for. He answered, tapping me on the shoulder, "You have all the abilities to be a fine speaker."

B. Goldgar, of course, really enjoyed my first taste of public speaking. He immediately became closer friends with me. After that he invited me to his house, *The Beast of Property* by Johann Most was the first book that Goldgar gave me to read. It is impossible to convey today the effect that the first anarchist pamphlet made on me.[21] Each of us can easily recall the tremendously deep impression made on us by that first pamphlet or speech which acquaints us with some sort of idealism. But it is interesting to note that my acquaintance with Goldgar spared me from having to first become familiar with socialism and instead brought me directly to the anarchist doctrine.

When I returned to Goldgar that first book which he had lent me (in Yiddish translation from German), he immediately gave me the still-famous treatise by Johann Most, *The God Pestilence*. The reader can himself imagine the effect that it had on me, a person who had recently studied rabbinics in a yeshiva. The third book that Goldgar gave me was *Let There Be Light* by Morris Winchevsky.

Once Goldgar took a few of us into the woods and presented for us in Yiddish a "disputation" between priest and rabbi, by Heinrich Heine,[22] which concludes with the famous sentence: *Dass sie alle beide stinken* (They both stink considerably).

One of the deepest impressions that I cannot forget to this day is about reading "The Trial of Ferdinand LaSalle and His Speech before the Court."

Throughout this period we prepared for the strike in Mr. Duke's factory. The strike was supposed to take place just after the end of the contract that Mr. Duke had made with us for the first six months.

In that very day, when the six months were up, we were all called in to Mr. Duke's office. The unexpected action caught us by surprise. We had no notion of what was going on.

Portraying himself as our "benefactor," Duke arose and addressed us as follows: "Sirs, your six-month contract with me is expired. Where do you want to go? Every married man will be given a free train ticket and twenty dollars, every unmarried man, a ticket and five dollars."

The surprise which that caused us is easy to imagine. We stood dumbstruck, not knowing what to answer or what to say. Before we had time to recover, we already had in hand the tickets together with the $20 or $5 gold pieces and we were soon out on the street.

For Goldgar and Lieberman this was a terrible disappointment. We, the workers, felt as if we lost something there. Gone were all the plans and hopes for a strike which was supposed to bring us prosperity and a more pleasant life. We were once again unemployed.

Mr. Duke, having found out about the plan for a strike in his factory, secretly began to make all the preparations to implement making cigarettes with machines instead of by hand. As soon as we left, Mr. Duke installed the machines and the mechanization broke—no, not broke but prevented our strike and my first chance at participation in a strike.[23] Mr. Duke and the machines were victorious over us. No union, all over and done with.

Disappointed and embittered, all of the imported workers packed up our meager belongings, left Durham and returned to New York.[24]

Reading through the pamphlets by Johann Most had a great effect on me and ignited in my soul a great revolutionary fire. The more I read his words, the more I revered Johann Most himself. When I came back to New York, my chief wish became to hear him speak. I didn't have to wait long. The following Sunday a debate took place between Johann Most and Alex Jonas on the topic: "Freedom for Education, or Education for Freedom." Most, of course, defended the former and the social democrat Jonas, the latter.[25]

To convey the manner in which Most spoke is impossible. Only those lucky enough to have heard him sometime will really understand the veracity of my claim. To say that Most could inspire an audience is not enough. He electrified, simply enchanted each listener, whether an adversary or a friend.

In a masterful speech, Johann Most analyzed the history of all the struggles which humanity had led and experienced. Every war of liberation of the enslaved brought with it the possibility and realization of more and more freedoms. Moreover, it is only logical that education as it is commonly understood and as we would like to see in reality can only happen through a complete liberation of the oppressed.

First, then, the liberation and the result of it: the opportunity for education for everyone.

Alexander Jonas, the German social democratic leader in America, challenged the entire doctrine of Most's arguments. Jonas' position was: freedom can only be achieved after the oppressed receive education. Jonas didn't demonstrate how workers can receive education without freedom. Consequently, Most emerged the moral victor in the debate.

The first speech I heard from Most, at the debate, had an enormous effect on me. It ignited my already simmering revolutionary soul. And to this day when I recall Johann Most, I hear in my ears his mighty voice which used to enchant me and all the workers present, exhorting and calling to the struggle against all forms of oppression. But where is the Johann Most of the current generation?

Once I happened to be in New York when Most and a group of our German comrades put on Gerhard Hauptmann's world-famous social drama *Die Weber*. I will never forget the impression that his acting had on me![26] It would suffice to

remember that the critics in all the New York newspapers who
were at the performance not only wrote enthusiastically about
his acting, but also explained that with this one role as he,
Most, portrayed it, he showed that he could have become the
most famous actor of the greatest stage.

Johann Most came into our movement from the social-
democrat camp. He played an important role in the Social
Democratic party in Germany. He was also a Social-Democratic
deputy in the German parliament in the time of the iron
Chancellor Bismarck. Comrade Most was also among the first
victims of Bismarck's anti-Socialist law. Until his last moment
he occupied himself with activities for our anarchist cause.
When death came to him in 1906, he was on a lecture tour, and
one can rightly say about Comrade Johann Most that he died
as he had lived, struggling for the anarchist cause. [27]

For those who never had the opportunity to hear Most, I
want to stress the significance of the role that Most and the
German movement played in the development of the anarchist
movement in America. The German anarchist workers, with
Most as writer and speaker, not only created a powerfully
influential German anarchist movement in America, but also
helped create a Jewish as well as an American anarchist
movement.

I had the good fortune to speak on the same stage as
Comrade Most one time at a Paris Commune commemoration
in New York, and a second time, at a Yom Kippur ball in the
same city.[28] My admiration and love for Most thus grew each
time I heard him speak. The topic could have been a scientific
one—he put in so much earnestness and fervor that it turned
into a speech which greatly captivated all the listeners.

The police in New York for Most's entire decades-long
activism treated him as a foreigner, in the brutal fashion. With
a foreigner, a representative of the law may of course do as he
pleases. What the police didn't know, or rather, didn't
understand is: if Johann Most had really wanted to incite the
masses (a charge which the police often brought against him,
these same upholders of the law, in their brutal attacks on
workers), New York would have had bloody riots.

I don't exaggerate one bit. Johann Most could so mesmerize his listeners that they would at any time go with him should he call them to man the barricades. He could bring the apathetic person to tears with his hypnotizing power.

The police hated him for enlightening the workers, and at every opportunity it was apparent what brutal dogs the state had made of them.

After the attempted assassination by Leon Czolgosz of President William McKinley, the police denounced Johann Most and managed to have him sent away for a year in prison on the "Black Island."[29] He was held in the same cell with Chinese, so that he wouldn't be able to agitate among the exiled Germans who might have been imprisoned together with him. In prison Johann Most continued to edit, as he had his whole life, the weekly anarchist organ *Die Freiheit.*

Johann Most was the greatest people's-agitator that the anarchist movement ever had, from the time I first participated in the movement to this very day. I do not have the slightest doubt of it. And if, during his life, a social revolution had broken out in America—Johann Most would have played the same role in it that M. Bakunin played in the lands where revolutions occurred in his time.[30]

Chapter 2

Returning to New York, I again went to work at cigar making. This time, fate brought me to work in a factory belonging to a Mrs. Stein. The factory was of the sort that was exceptional even in those days. Mrs. Stein used to boast to each new worker who came to work for her, "With me you can work when you want and as long as you want!" And this was no exaggeration because the factory was never locked. The workers who worked for her were just as strange as this Mrs. Stein and her factory. The cripples from all over the city, workers who liked to drink, workers whose home was the harbor where the ships docked—these were the workers in Mrs. Stein's cigar factory. Mrs. Stein paid out the wages twice a day. Don't be alarmed if this sounds too good to be true. Before lunch she gave a quarter and before supper fifty cents. We used to make four to five dollars a week. Getting paid twice a day was the main attraction for the sort of worker who worked for her and likewise for the provider, Mrs. Stein. It was a very appropriate match. Of course, I couldn't stay long in such a paradise. At a chance encounter, a man considerately offered me the opportunity to take out a union book for three dollars, and so I immediately joined the union.

The union sent me to a union shop. The wages were very different than with Mrs. Stein. Not four or five, but ten dollars a week. Also, the shop was not open twenty-four hours a day, but eight hours. That was the workday. Like every newcomer, I immediately broke the union rules, working a few minutes after 12:00. And right after work I was invited to the union office. There I was brought before the union court. My apologizing and explaining that this was the first time in my life that I trespassed a union principle was to no avail. The sentence was: union rules must be upheld. I was fined three dollars. I was actually pretty angry. I paid up, but after all, in truth, they really were right.

While Mr. Duke had prevented our planned strike from taking place in North Carolina, this meant that my first experience with a strike would take place in New York. But this time as well, I was not actually a striker. Five thousand cigar makers did strike, but I worked in a union shop. I merely paid a percentage of my wages to help carry out the strike.

One time, at a strikers' meeting, a man asked to speak. He was given the floor, and when he got it, he started trying to convince the strikers that with a strategy of sitting around in the halls and eating sandwiches, drinking beer and dancing a little, they would never win the strike. What must be done, he said, is to go to the boss, chase him out of the office and take over the factory. The chairman answered him that it was a wonderfully nice idea for the future when all the workers would be perfectly enlightened. However, carrying this out now in every manufacturing industry would be a dangerous idea and this was not the time or place. A year after the strike, we found out from the union that the man who had given the clever advice was a spy-provocateur. We soon convinced him not only to leave the cigar trade, but to leave America as well.

The leaders of the Cigar Makers' Union at that time were Stopper and Yablonovski, both Jews. Samuel Gompers was then working at making cigars in a Spanish shop.

The city with its factories, the tumult of people running at every turn, exerted on me a desire to leave the factory and go back to nature in the countryside.

At that time, while my thoughts were working out plans to leave the city, a young man was staying with me, Jack Bayuk (now the millionaire owner of Bayuk Bros. cigars in Philadelphia).[31] His father, Moyshe Bayuk was a *landsman* of mine from Tshekhanovtse. There isn't even any reason to be proud of my fellow countryman, because while still on the other side of the ocean, he had already done six months in prison for a false business deal.

The German Jews had a fund to save the "common" Jews from business and help them to become farmers in America. And they also gave land to Moyshe Bayuk. As soon as Jack Bayuk found out that I wanted to buy a farm, he wrote to his father to ask his advice about it. It just then happened, to my misfortune, that a rich American landowner near Moyshe's

farm had fifty-seven acres of land to sell. Moyshe Bayuk sent
me a letter right away with an invitation to come and look over
the large estate, saying that a real fortune is waiting for us.

When we arrived in Carmel, New Jersey, lunch was waiting
for us.[32] Moyshe Bayuk immediately started to dissuade us
from buying the farm. First of all, he said, the farmer is not
honest. He remembered that he had written us that we could
buy the farm for five or six dollars an acre. Now he actually
wanted seventeen dollars for each acre of land. Which was a
sign that it was really an estate. So we really should buy it.

After lunch we were brought in a carriage to look at the
farm. Moyshe picked up a handful of dirt and called out to me,
"You see how the earth crumbles in my fist? That shows what
good soil it is." As soon as he had said that, I sank into a
muddy swamp. Moyshe didn't give up, and he immediately
declared, "If I had such land, I would be a millionaire!
Cranberries grow here!"

I asked him, "How many?"

"A hundred bushels for each acre of land," he answered,
"and you get five dollars a bushel now."

I became confused by the fortune in front of me. I began to
believe that I would soon be a millionaire. Moyshe promised
me another fortune from the estate: cedar trees. There are, he
told me, about two thousand of them. One can sell them for five
dollars a tree. My head started spinning, trying to figure my
future profits. We agreed on the terms of fifteen dollars an acre
and moved out of New York to Carmel.

To describe our life on the farm is not necessary: we all
slaved away. We worked making cigars in the city in order to
be able to maintain the great fortune that Mr. Moyshe Bayuk
so nicely outlined for us. There was a lot, an awful lot, which he
didn't mention. For example, we found out through bitter
experience, that cranberries really can grow in a swamp, and
one can actually get five dollars a bushel for them; however, it
requires thousands of dollars to cultivate the land so that it can
begin to yield cranberries. Likewise, for the second fortune
from the estate: the cedar trees. There was indeed a large
quantity of them, and a cedar tree was indeed worth five

dollars in those days. But Moyshe Bayuk forgot one small
detail: he forgot to mention that it takes seventy-five years for
a cedar tree to reach its full height.

Eventually it became clear to us why Mr. Moyshe Bayuk
and his son, Jack, advised so strongly against buying the farm.
That was the means they employed to influence me to want to
buy it. In addition, the role that the father and son played with
the farmer, as the farmer later told us, was also not
untarnished. They told him to demand seventeen dollars an
acre, when in reality, he had asked for seven dollars. The best
part is that they were both such sly businessmen, that he, the
farmer, didn't even collect the seven dollars an acre. They took
every penny that I paid out.

It should also be mentioned here that in the period that I
bought the estate, I met one of those personages about whom
one reads in books, but seldom meets. This was a young man,
Bacall. He was very immersed in philosophy and anarchism.
He was also a vegetarian, a deep-thinking man. And his life
was sadly cut short by the proletarian disease, consumption.
He maintained a distrust of both Bayuks from the very first
moment he met them. (He made us all swear before his death
that we wouldn't let Mr. Bayuk touch his dead body.) He was
not mistaken, as it turned out. So that's how my anticipated
"golden fortune" from the land ended up. After two years of
slaving away, I had to leave the farm as it stood and return to
the city.

After leaving Carmel, this time I didn't go back to New
York, but to a new city, Philadelphia. I once again went back to
making cigars. At that time, a committee from the bakery
workers came to me. Labowitz was the spokesman for the
committee. They came to me for help organizing the bakery
workers in Philadelphia.

It would seem strange and unbelievable if I were to describe
today the conditions under which bakery workers had to work
in those days. It is, however, the truth. It was like this: they
worked sixteen hours a day. Every Thursday, they worked a
full twenty-four hours in order to prepare the *shabes khale*.[33]

Wages were at the discretion of the owner, from three to ten dollars a week.

I immediately agreed to help. We called the first meeting at Second and Catherine Streets. When I began speaking, there were about thirty bakers, and they were so exhausted that half of them were asleep, including the chairman. Of course, my speech woke them up a little. (In the cellars where the bakers used to work in those days, there wasn't even a staircase, and more than once we managed by going around from cellar to cellar and pulling them out with a rope to attend the meeting.) They began coming to the meetings called by the union. Thus was the foundation laid for the first Jewish bakers' union in Philadelphia. That was far from the end of my involvement with the bakery workers union in Philadelphia, but more about that later.

I am still not sure to this very day whether Mahlon Barnes,[34] the leader of the American Cigar Makers' Union, did or did not know about my small achievement with the Jewish bakery workers. In any case, one day he sent someone to ask me to try and organize the Jewish cigar makers in a union. I explained to him that the Jewish workers were unable to pay twenty-five cents a week for dues. I could only try to organize a local with ten cents dues. Barnes agreed to my plan. At the second meeting there were already 120 Jewish cigar makers. After that, feeling more self-assured, I sent for Barnes, proposed and then defended the usefulness of joining the national corporation of the cigar makers' union. My suggestion was accepted. Thus the foundation was likewise laid for the first Jewish cigar makers' union.

Unexpectedly, I received a telegram from Joseph Barondess telling me to come to New York immediately, because the entire cloakmakers' union was about to go under. I emphasize the word unexpected, because just nine months previously, ten thousand cloakmakers had marched on May Day in the streets of New York! A parade for which special, festive costumes and flags had been made. And the two leaders, Braff and Garside,[35] led the parade, a parade that threw the whole American capitalist press into a panic. The press was terrified that social revolution in America was imminent—and right after that, such a telegram![36] But such was the fate of many, many Jewish unions and other social movements in America. They arose suddenly, and with a pop were extinguished, like the flame from a burning candle.

Arriving in New York, I sought out the office of the cloakmakers' union. It was in a basement in the Lower East Side, where air and sunshine were a rarity. Seated on one side of the table I found Barondess, the organizer at that time. On the other side was Kuntz, the secretary.[37] On the walls hung large pictures of Karl Marx and Ferdinand LaSalle. Between the two pictures was a picture of a cloakmaker who had been recently arrested. In a corner were two boxes of the special caps which had been made and worn at the aforementioned parade. Barondess and Kuntz, sitting in that office, looked as if a dead person had just been carried out of there and they were sitting shiva for him. There was no question of paying the rent; it had already been two months since the rent had been paid. If they got really deep in debt, they would raffle a watch and thus pay the rent. Dues, which were always a sore point with Jewish workers, were then ten cents a week. Even that, it seems, was too much for them.

Naturally, the condition of the union office reflected the condition of the cloakmaker in those days. The well known sweatshop system was then in full bloom. They worked in every tenement house, some in an unventilated room and some in a dark, airless basement. And the meager wages were barely enough to live on. The union was, naturally, as good as useless at being able to enact changes or improvements in the factories, let alone in tenement sweatshop holes. The only time the workers were able to squeeze anything out of the bosses was at the height of the season. It was not even deemed necessary to ask the union if one should strike or not. Workers got together, declared a strike, led it for a week or two, and sometimes won and sometimes lost. In most of the cases, the union didn't even know about the strikes.

The meeting about which Barondess had sent me a telegram was to take place in the evening. As I had arrived in the daytime, and it was already evening, Barondess invited me to his house. When we arrived, his wife was doing the laundry. The look on her face told me that I was not a welcome guest. I noticed that they held a silent consultation. The decision was to bring a whole herring with bread and a glass of tea to wash it down. After that exalted meal,[38] we both went to the Valhalla Hall on Orchard Street, where the meeting was supposed to take place. To our surprise, the hall was already packed. Hundreds of workers couldn't get in. To describe the enthusiasm, it will suffice to note that over eight hundred workers signed up for the union at that meeting. It was from that foundation that the later mighty cloakmakers' union was strengthened and grew.

My own excitement from the meeting was also not negligible. I remember, to this very day, my parting words to Barondess. "Whenever you need me, just ask and I'll come," I said to him.

One of the organizers of the men's tailors' union, which belonged to the United Garment Workers union, was Meyer Sheinfeld. Meyer Sheinfeld's appearance was such that you would sooner take him for a saloon keeper than a union organizer. He wanted to carry out a mass meeting of the pants makers in Baltimore. It just so happened, that he missed his train. A delegation came to me in a hurry, to ask me to take his place, which I did.

A few hours later, he came to me with a bunch of people to thank me for helping him out. He sent someone to buy beer and started recounting those frequent adventures, how they used to organize unions among Jewish workers.

This happened, Sheinfeld related, in a time when the men's tailor union was bankrupt, powerless. Workers were starving. Sheinfeld went and called a meeting of twenty healthy pressers, the sort who could strike a blow if necessary. The twenty were divided into three delegations, each of which would go from shop to shop. Work started at 5:00 in the morning and was finished before nightfall. There was no question of allowing any pressers to be left out. The other workers were not a concern. If you take out all the pressers, the shop has to stop. They started bringing the pressers into the union office on Bruce Street. One might imagine that several hundred pressers were taken away from work. Sheinfeld assured us that four thousand pressers were taken away from work to join the union! And the bosses started running to the union to settle. The best part, Sheinfeld said, accompanied by a resounding burst of laughter, was that the workers themselves didn't know why they were suddenly out on strike. After the victorious conclusion of the strike, he was carried around on people's hands. They bought him a gold watch. "Now he has what to eat; now there's a union." Three or four years later I heard that the founder of the aforementioned pressers union was finally in his proper place—a saloon keeper.

Chapter 3

The Debaters Club[39]

Everyone today is familiar with the important role that the debates played in the development of the social and political movement in this country. The first organization which attracted me sufficiently to join was a debating club whose guiding spirit was a man named Baker. The main questions which were debated there were religion, economy and philosophy. Discussions were held twice a week. Membership cost twenty-five cents a month. It was also at the debating club that I became acquainted with the history of the cooperative experiments, which were led by Robert Owen and Saint-Simon. Becoming acquainted with this work had an enormous effect on many of us. The effect on me personally will be seen in the further experiences which portray the experimental attempts at cooperation among the Jewish workers in America.

With the Knights of Liberty, the history of the Jewish anarchist movement in Philadelphia truly began. The group was founded by workers. Its leading spirit was a man by the name of Goldstein, a recently arrived radical-atheist from England.[40] The group's first meeting took place at the home of a fellow named Rittenberg, on Catherine Street.[41] At the first meeting some twenty people were gathered. The majority of us didn't have a clear idea what we wanted, other than the fact that we were all atheists. In those days, in America as well as England, the atheist movement was very influential. In particular, it left deep tracks and led to the development of all the radical and political movements. If we, meaning the majority of the group, didn't know exactly what we wanted, aside from "atheism," there was one fellow who did know quite clearly, not only what he wanted, but also for what purpose he became an active member and always let us use his house for meetings. This was the aforementioned Mr. Rittenberg. This same Jew was blessed with five daughters. Five daughters for a Jew: this alone would have been a misfortune, even if they

had been personable and good-looking. Mr. Rittenberg had to
have a doubly good fortune: five daughters, each one uglier
than the next. This Mr. Rittenberg, however, understood the
business; how could he more easily marry off his five "beauties"
than in this circle where the people were more preoccupied
with ideas and plans for the future than with the reality on
earth? And in truth, he was not mistaken. He managed to give
away all five, and, of course, after that we never saw his face
again. The Knights of Liberty lost more than they gained from
Mr. Rittenberg's prize. The group was growing and used to
exercise more and more influence on the workers in
Philadelphia. The lectures, which we gave frequently, were
better and better attended. So we were forced to move to a
larger place, 203 Pine Street.

The dues were five cents a week. Every new member used
to receive a card valid for fifty-two weeks. Each week a hole
was punched. One of my sister's daughters came to me once
with a membership card and asked me with the naïveté of a
greenhorn (which she was), "So, when you have punched out
the whole card, I won't have to go to work anymore?"

We had a lot of speakers in the group. We had one Gretch, a
talmudist and main atheist speaker.[42] Aside from being
learned, he was also a thinker and a deeply-convincing orator.
Now he is already dead. A second speaker was Telson, who is
now a Communist. Prenner was a newly-arrived speaker, a
member of the New York group Pioneers of Liberty.[43] Prenner
was twenty-two years old. His oratory was very lively and was
distinguished by its beautiful speech. He was a cigar maker by
trade, well-read in Russian, a sort of semi-intellectual.[44] With
his settling in Philadelphia and becoming a member of our
group, he caused the Knights of Liberty to openly declare itself
to be an "anarchist-communist group."

With the transformation of the Knights of Liberty into an
"anarchist group," there began the glorious period of the
Jewish-anarchist movement in Philadelphia. The group began
to hold lectures every week with speakers from New York. We
brought down from New York: Dr. J. Maryson,[45] Weichsel,
Wilentshik, Girdzhansky, R. Lewis (then the editor of the

Fraye Arbeter Shtime), Staller, R. Liebert, Wilson, A. Schneider, Weinberg,[46] A. Kansa, Michael Cohn,[47] Moshe Katz, David Edelstat, Sarah Edelstat (his sister). The German speakers which we used to bring down were: Strumpen,[48] Zelig, and Johann Most. Various other Philadelphia speakers were also becoming more numerous. We already had: Dr. Gordon,[49] Dr. Staller, Dr. Barbour,[50] Prenner, Gretch and myself.

When the Knights of Liberty group existed, we often used to hold meetings in private homes, at members' homes. Once at such a meeting, at the home of Comrade Staller,[51] two people knocked on the door and explained that they wanted to come inside and make an important suggestion to us. We bade them to come in. Both of them had pockets stuffed with literature. And right after they came in they began handing out small pamphlets to everyone. The pamphlet was about the single tax movement (property taxes). Having done that, they began to present their plan. They explained that we will never bring about anarchism with pamphlets. It requires concrete action. First, all the workers from every trade must be organized. If each one would give just one dollar a week (at that time there were fifty thousand workers in Philadelphia), then in one year we can amass $250,000. With such a huge sum we could immediately proceed to the work. And the work would consist of building houses for the workers who had joined. Workers would see that working people really have good houses, and the organization will thus grow, such that we can begin to produce clothing and food for our own use.

And our deep-thinking comrade, Robert Wilson, got up and asked those who brought the plan this question:

"Assuming that your plan is good, we proceed and begin building the first houses; if it happens to turn out that I am not one of the last thousand of the fifty thousand workers in Philadelphia, rather my number is merely 5000: how many years will I have to wait until it is my turn to get a house?"

"I am afraid it would be minimum a hundred years. It is unfortunately no more than a utopia, although it pains me to say it..." And the two single-taxers went away, presumably very dissatisfied.

In those days, the Jewish workers to all intents and purposes didn't know that there existed such a thing as social democrats. This arose from the fact that most of the Jewish unions were exclusively founded by anarchists. It is not necessary to emphasize that the social democrats didn't derive any great pleasure from that. Not only did they resent us, but they actually decided to destroy what they called the "Anarchist Gibraltar of Philadelphia." They started firing their artillery at us. They brought Louis Miller, Morris Hillquit, Abe Cahan, Michael Zametkin and Benjamin Feigenbaum.[52] The struggle between us and them flared up and the outcome was that they, the social democrats, beat us. They took over the reigns of the Jewish unions and hold on to them till this very day.

Later I will have to give typical examples of the methods employed by the leading spirits of the social democrats in order to beat us, the anarchists.

The atheist propaganda which we carried out in Philadelphia was obviously very offensive to religious Jews. One day, a Jew came to me and explained to me that his name was Mr. Berger, and he was coming as a representative of the Jews of Philadelphia, who had held a meeting and decided to send him to have a talk with me, the president of the unbelievers. And he started to plead with me: "You know of all the torments and troubles which the Jews put up with all over the world, and now there is a land in the world which opens its arms wide to us, such a golden land, America. Then you come with your unbelievers and make a mockery and a disgrace of it all, endangering the entire Jewish people in America."

Having heard out his splendid sermon, I asked him what he wanted. He wanted me, the "president," to let him come and give a moralizing lecture to our group, and he would show all of us that we are not following the right path.

Hearing his wish, I gave him more than he asked for. Why should he speak only to our group? We would print up handbills, give him our Sunday hall and have him speak to all of our sympathizers. Mr. Berger was agreeable and requested he be allowed to come speak dressed in rabbinical garb. I consented to that: if it's going to be a performance, let's have the whole kit and caboodle, that is, in theater-speech, with all the scenery.

Mr. Berger was in love with the daughter of a Jewish worker, someone named Burstein. When he came and told them that he was going to speak dressed as a rabbi, they laughed at him. That spoiled a little his anticipation of triumph. He arrived with Burstein's daughter as a singer comes to the opera, but without the rabbinical attire. The hall was packed.

I opened the meeting and gave all the details which led to Mr. Berger's coming to speak to us. And I introduced Mr. Berger. He began his lecture quoting biblical passages, and each verse was delivered by him with mistakes. From Hebrew he sprang to Russian and started citing with just as many mistakes. Then he finished up in like fashion quoting from German. It turned out that, while speaking, he had already sensed his failure and wanted to leave immediately. I asked him to sit until we could give him our response.

The first to have a word was our talmudist, Comrade Gretch. In a bitter speech, full of sarcasm, he dissected Berger's error-laden lecture, ending with the words, "Among 10,000 Jews there couldn't be found any other to come save the Jewish people from us, the unbelievers, than a person who knows no Hebrew, no Russian, and no German." Then Telson began to prove to him that his grammar was so faulty that he couldn't even have completed Russian elementary school.

Mr. Berger endeavored to leave after each speech, and each time I called out, "Mr. Berger, please hear out our response to your lecture." Finally, he freed himself, embarrassed, forgetting about the girl for whom he had come to show off. Not only did he lose the opportunity to save us for the Jewish people, and the Jewish people from our danger, but he also lost his beloved, Burstein's daughter.

It is interesting to note that a couple of years later, at a meeting with Johann Most, I saw a Jew standing and warmly applauding Most's speech. He seemed very familiar to me; I looked closely and, lo and behold, it was the same Mr. Berger.

"What's going on?" I asked him.

"Well, he's right," he answered. I had no further encounters with Mr. Berger.

Many people who write or speak today about Yom Kippur balls with a view to repeating such ventures under the auspices of the communists, do not know that the balls began not only on account of the anarchists. The truth is this: from the beginning, both had the practice, the anarchists as well as the social democrats. How many people know the fact that the late Philip Krantz used to march around every Yom Kippur in the Whitechapel streets in London with a large cake? One should also recall that Jewish socialists and anarchists were first atheists.

When our Philadelphia group Knights of Liberty consisted of 120 members, there arose the question of Yom Kippur. Then we realized what kind of a crowd we had with us. The question came up: seeing that the Jewish religion stood in the way of the labor movement, we should make a ball on Yom Kippur, thus weakening the effect of the religion. The discussion concerning a Yom Kippur ball lasted three weeks. Some maintained that that sort of propaganda would do us more harm than good; it would make us reviled by the faithful. The other side believed just the opposite. The feat of a Yom Kippur ball would interest a lot of people and they would know who we are and what we want.

The discussion ended with a compromise: On Yom Kippur lectures would be held, not balls. Of course, the lectures would have to be anti-religious. Gretch, our talmudist, had his life in danger a whole year. His lectures on "Khumash mit seykhl"[53] made him hated, but also known and loved by the population of Philadelphia. It got to the point that after each of his lectures, about ten of us had to accompany him home. His speeches always had an effect. That was really the main reason for the anger from the side of the religious Jews.

Comrade Prenner and Comrade Gordon, who were the main leaders of our group, began to quarrel. It ended up with a split in the group. There were two factions. The Knights of Liberty held their meetings at Tenth and South Streets, and the new group, "The New Generation" held theirs at Third and Gaskill Streets.[54]

Our attendees were not overly concerned by the split. As proof of this, most of those present at the daytime meetings used to, take sandwiches out of their pockets after the meeting, eat them up, and go into the second hall instead of going home. To such a degree was the audience in those days interested in ideas.

There was also another motive in having the two groups, which was to take advantage of an opportunity to capture the listeners of those who used to hold their meetings at Third and Gaskill Streets. That angered the social democrats, who then began bringing all their VIPs from New York.

Chapter 4

The propaganda which we anarchists carried out in Philadelphia was, aside from being social-economic and political, also anti-religious. Our propaganda had attracted a lot of attention, especially in high society of the wealthier Jews, who were mainly German Yahudim.[55] The more followers the radical movement gained, the more it became a thorn in their side. We felt their hatred and fury from every side. Virtually none of us, however, could imagine the devilish plan which they thought up to effectively destroy the radical movement in Philadelphia.

Suddenly, like thunder before a storm, Isidore Prenner, Moscowitz, M. Gillis and Jacobson were arrested.[56] At first, nobody knew the charges. At the hearing, everything became clear to us: it turned out that the well-known Jewish philanthropist, Simon Mayer, had thought up and arranged the entire "frame-up" of those arrested. Simon Mayer didn't just carry out the "philanthropical frame-up" for no particular reason. It's true that our general propaganda was one of the factors which led to the persecutions by denunciation. But this was not all. There was also an economic motive: Mayer was a close friend of the famous cloak manufacturer Blum, against whom Prenner and Staller carried out a strike of six-months' duration.[57] From that strike, Mr. Blum lost tens of thousands of dollars. He almost went bankrupt. And they wanted to send Prenner away, more than any of the others. First a Jew came up and gave testimony and swore that he heard Comrade Prenner say in a speech that we must slaughter all the capitalists and take a bath in their blood; he saw Comrade Moscowitz (the aforementioned current president of a khevre-kedisha) as he attacked a gray-haired Jew and hit him with a set of tefillin, of all things.[58] He heard Comrade Jacobson tell workers on a cold winter's day, "You walk around frozen and naked, while the windows of Strawbridge and Clothier's department store are full of clothes. Go and break the glass and get yourselves some warm clothes."

Of M. Gillis he swore that he was the very same man who rented the hall where all the revolutionary speeches took place. Simply put, the point of the denunciation indictment was treason against the state, and the whole order which upholds it, in order for the state to punish the "Buntovshtshiks." It is not easy to describe the impression which the indictment first made on us. Now, decades after it happened, it would still sound to us like a second-rate comedy. It was all so unbelievable. Slowly, however, the seriousness of the "frame-up" became clear to all of us. And one can imagine how anxious we were about it. We awaited the trial with impatience

As soon as the trial got underway,[59] a lawyer got up and demanded a separate trial for his client, M. Gillis, on the grounds that he was not an anarchist like the others, but rather a social democrat. (M. Gillis is now a contributor to the *Forverts*.) The prosecutor did not think long and immediately opposed, and the logic of his argument was "iron-clad:" Since the color of the flags in the halls of both groups is red, this is proof that social democrats and anarchists are one and the same. And the logic of the prosecutor won out. The court of capital did not want to separate the anarchists from the Social Democrats.

Our witness was Forvein. His appearance was exactly as our enemies imagine a typical revolutionary, with long hair and shabby clothes. The prosecutor started right in with him. He thundered, "Who is he? Where was he born? He comes from Siberia?" Not satisfied, it seems, with his exclamations, he asked Forvein, "Do you believe in God?" Forvein took out a packet of papers from his pocket and wanted to read aloud. The prosecutor asked him, "You want to give us a lecture? That you can do at the Friendship Liberal League! (an English-speaking atheist organization, which still exists today).[60] Answer me, do you or do you not believe in God?" Forvein answered, "No."— "That is enough for me," said the prosecutor. Then our beloved and always active (now deceased) Natasha Notkin was brought before the court. The cross examination began:

Prosecutor: Where are you from?
Natasha: From Russia.

Prosecutor: When did you cut off your hair?
Natasha: In Russia.
Prosecutor: Are you a Nihilist?
Natasha: I don't know what that is.[61]

The treatment that our witnesses received from the prosecutor is evident from these extracts, which remain in my memory until today. Instead of easing the situation, the appearance of our witnesses throughout the prosecutor's cross-examination aggravated the charge. (The defense was Pentecost, the former and present lawyer and later anarchist for a time.)[62] The atmosphere in the courtroom was charged with hatred toward the "foreigners."

Our lawyer, with all of his speeches, could not wipe away the hatred created by the prosecutor, especially when he began his closing argument, which I remember by heart. He began to describe the most important moments from the French Revolution and passionately cried out, "In that period of the French Revolution the Robespierres and Marats slaughtered thousands of the best citizens!" And as for the point that the defense had brought a professor who testified that one of the accused, Prenner, had been the best student at Temple University, to this the prosecutor answered: That only shows that he learned to be a revolutionary at the expense of our citizens. "And this same Prenner, who stands before you—this Nihilist, were he given the chance, wouldn't he carry out the same slaughter on our best citizens in America?[63] What all the accused want here in this country is a French Revolution! Find them guilty—stop their devilish plans. Show thus your true patriotism for the fatherland in a critical time. This decisive moment stands before us all now as never before in the whole history of America."

And the good "citizens" of the court understood the danger to the "fatherland" and did their duty: they helped to complete the frame-up of the accused. The verdict was as prepared and expected: all were found guilty, even Gillis the social democrat. The sentence was one year in prison for each.

The sentence brought forth a storm of protests in all parts of the city and throughout the land. Even the perpetrators of the frame-up began to feel very uncomfortable as victors over us. And once again, the philanthropist, Mr. Mayer, interceded and got the sentence commuted to eight months in jail. Before that happened, rumors began to fly that Mr. Mayer had begun sending messengers to Prenner. They pleaded with him: why should he lay down his life, suffering and wasting away in prison? With his talent for speaking and his leadership abilities, he could become quite an important figure, if only he would come to his senses.

And to our great regret and astonishment, the messengers slowly began to influence Prenner. After his liberation, he distanced himself from us right away, began studying, and later finished his studies in law and engineering. [64] While those sentenced were doing their time in prison, our group supported their families. Moscowitz's wife received four dollars a week from us. She also received, to our knowledge, an additional four dollars a week from the Single-Taxers—all together eight dollars, which is more than her husband ever earned working in a shop.

Chapter 5

I already related how the pamphlets describing the experiments of Robert Owen and Saint-Simon were read with great interest. Some years later, when Sh. Peskin returned from a trip to England, he published a series of articles in the *Forverts* enthusiastically describing the wonderful cooperative movement organized by the workers in England. Under the influence of Sh. Peskin's articles, I got together with five or six young people and we began diligently reading and studying all of the English literature we could obtain on the cooperative movement. Our enthusiasm increased and we, though few in number, began to dream about a cooperative movement which would embrace the entire Jewish labor movement in Philadelphia. The first thing we did was to call a meeting of those workers we remembered had shown some degree of sympathy and interest in a cooperative movement. The meeting was in a small hall; 25 people attended.

I opened the meeting and began explaining the goal we had undertaken, and the rationale behind it. I said, "There is no sense in continually carrying on an economic struggle exclusively in the domain of production. We are exploited in the factories. But from the miserable fifth we receive as wages, we are just as exploited, or better put, robbed, in the realm of consumption.[65] Therefore the struggle in the realm of consumption is just as necessary. We view the boss of the factory as an enemy. Well, what about the storekeeper? He also makes money from our labor, so doesn't that make him just as much the enemy? The manufacturer robs us from one side and the storekeeper from the other. We are squeezed by both of them equally. We must therefore lay the foundation for a cooperative movement. And our goal should be to get the workers used to being cooperators in the realm of consumption. And later, also becoming partners in the economic realm as producers. What this means in reality is this: through the union in the realm of production and through the cooperatives in the realm of consumption, the liberation of the worker can and will come."

After my speech and other briefer remarks, the first Jewish cooperative organization in America was founded at that meeting. And, as usual, with an English name: The Workers Cooperative Society.[66] The newly-established cooperative movement declared right from the beginning that it was, and strived to be, a non-partisan workers movement, where workers from all political persuasions and directions would be able to take part. We began to call mass meetings with speakers from New York and Philadelphia. We, the directors, were actually nonpartisan. We invited everybody to speak— anybody who wanted to come to us. As far as I remember, the first speakers at the meeting were: Louis Miller, William Feigenbaum, Meyer London, Voltairine de Cleyre, Emma Goldman, Moyshe Katz and almost all of our then-active Philadelphia comrades.[67]

Our sincere attempt to run the cooperative movement, as a nonpartisan organization, was immediately dealt its first blow from the social democrats. Because I was the founder and principal active member in the cooperative movement, it was promptly labeled an anarchist movement. However, the workers ignored the social democratic boycott, and began to come into our ranks by the hundreds. It wasn't long before we had a thousand members. It is unnecessary to describe the enthusiasm and joy among us, the founders. One can easily imagine it. Our propaganda was further carried out in the same spirit of nonpartisanship as before. We invited Eugene V. Debs to come and speak to us. Although Debs was unable to come, to our great delight he sent along a letter of greeting, in which he reassured us that we were on the right track. First, he wrote, you have a national movement, which will eventually lead to an international movement.

Debs' letter of approval struck the Philadelphia social democrats like a bombshell. They hadn't expected it. As a result of the letter, they ceased holding propaganda meetings directed against the cooperative movement as an anarchist group. Furthermore, they gradually began joining the cooperative movement. With great enthusiasm, we honored them in our choice of M. Gillis as president of the organization.[68] We decided that the membership fee would be $2.50 in the cooperative and another $2.50 per member when the time came to initiate important ventures, that is, when we had $2000 in the cashbox.

This very question brought us to lengthy and stormy debates. We settled on a compromise: given that America is a land where the Jewish worker is only in the shop temporarily, and leaves the proletariat at the first opportunity, therefore only lawyers, rabbis and manufacturers will be barred from becoming members. Many of our members also began to demand that we open a cooperative store without delay and not wait until we had $2000 (as had been agreed). Many used the expression, "Strike while the iron is hot." As a result, not taking into account that we had to send a person out among the members to collect the quarter a week, and even with a "collector" we didn't receive the contribution from half of our members, despite all that, we proceeded to open a cooperative store with the $1000 already collected.

We decided to start with shoes for the obvious reason that everybody has to have shoes. It didn't take long for our troubles to begin. The first obstacle arose, the focal point—and partially the breaking point of the whole cooperative venture, and this was—getting union-made shoes! After all, we couldn't very well start a cooperative store with shoes made in a scab shop. The store manager started running around looking for union shoes. And he only found the sort of union shoes used by rough workers for the heaviest and muddiest work, shoes that weighed 3-4 times as much as ordinary shoes. Finally, we found out that we could obtain union shoes, but not in Philadelphia—in Boston. In those days the shipping costs were extremely high compared to today. But we had no other choice. Despite the extra costs, we had to import shoes from Boston.

The store opening was a festive day for us, and a great event in the labor movement in Philadelphia. The first week we literally sold out the entire inventory of $600 worth of shoes. Since it was difficult for us to obtain shoes, workers waited for

weeks for their turn to have the right to buy a pair of shoes in
the cooperative store. When we discovered the enthusiasm with
which the workers responded to and supported the first
cooperative venture, we quickly decided to take on another
article—hats.

You can imagine my own excitement about our success from
the fact that I came to a meeting of our cooperative society and
suggested that we open a banking division in our store. The
workers were saving their few dollars in capitalist banks,
which used the money for various purposes that helped further
retain the current order; better they should save their money
with us. Thereby, they would accomplish two things: we would
have the means to run the movement, and they would receive
payout in interest. Many of us simply didn't believe that such
idealistic plans could ever come to fruition. And remarkably,
the more my fantasy filled me with enthusiasm about all of the
fabulous plans, the more successfully each new enterprise was
realized. The banking division also began to be a success. Over
75 workers became depositors.

I cannot begin to estimate how far the branches of our
enterprise would have grown, assuming, of course, that
everything had continued as in the first five months of the
store's existence. You may be assured, however, that the
success and enthusiasm which this elicited among the Jewish
workers was such that the movement could have developed into
a gigantic cooperative organization beyond our wildest dreams.
That the cooperative movement was successful for us roused
great anger, hatred and fear among the storekeepers. Our
success, they understood, was their downfall. Therefore, they
became our sworn enemies and began looking for any means to
discredit us. They, our enemies, began spreading rumors about
us. With that they gradually began to accomplish their goal.
And this was the most significant factor in our subsequent
downfall. Every idealistic movement can only be successful as
long as the fullest measure of trust pervades within its own
ranks and outside of its ranks. Everything that is done and
implemented must be done and implemented in the most
honest manner. If, however, there is the smallest reason to

begin to doubt it, then the "worm" of doubt creeps in and continues to eat up every bit of confidence which remain, and everything ends up in chaos and disappointment.

Our secretary and treasurer was Bornstein, a devoted, active member of the S.L.P. (Socialist Labor Party). He was one of our most active members and also one of the most beloved. When we wanted to make him president, he stood up and announced solemnly that he was declining. "What, I should take a worker's money!"

Suddenly, things began happening in the finance division of the store, which immediately led us to suspect Bornstein. We hired an accountant and he found out that several hundred dollars was missing. It turned out that Bornstein had, with the same zeal with which he had thrown himself into our cooperative movement, also thrown himself into love affairs with young ladies. And this sort of affair had so disoriented the idealist that he began to take money from the cooperative treasury. The discovery struck all of us like thunder. Most of us didn't even begin to fathom how severely the event would affect morale and would finally lead to the collapse of all of our dreams.

Our enemies, the storekeepers, immediately spread a rumor throughout the city that Bornstein, the secretary-treasurer of the cooperative store, had seized several thousand dollars. We explained that we knew and that it was several hundred dollars, but to no avail. The main thing was that one of the "idealists" from the cooperative movement had embezzled money from the till.

How difficult it is to build something up, how much effort and sacrifice are expended on it! Whoever has, either alone or with others, helped to build something, will understand what I mean. But how fast it all comes to naught when it starts to founder! We, the principal active ones, didn't understand, to tell the truth, that all such efforts which we made after what happened with Bornstein were doomed to failure. We couldn't recover the trust and faith which had been there earlier.

One of the opponents of the cooperative was A. L. Wolfson, a contributor to the *Forverts*.[69] Once, Wolfson came into the

store and requested a pair of shoes. Edelstein, the store
manager, selected a pair of shoes for him. At that time Wolfson
was a life insurance agent, who walked miles day in and day
out. Since shoes have a tendency to pinch when new, especially
on the first few days they are worn, the cooperative's shoes
were no different. They didn't show any favoritism; they
pinched Wolfson, the humorist and opponent of cooperatives,
exactly the same as they would have pinched us, the supporters
of cooperatives. A couple of days after Wolfson bought the
shoes, he came into the store claiming that he could not wear
the shoes because they pinched. Well, you know what a shoe
store does in such a case: they stretch out the shoes. Wolfson
said no, cooperative shoes shouldn't be stretched: they simply
must not pinch. So what did he want?—a new pair of shoes. He
was asked to come to the meeting. A discussion got underway.
He only wanted new shoes. Some of the directors said to give
him a dollar refund, some said two dollars, and some said we
should give him new shoes. Finally we decided to give him back
a dollar. Wolfson refused it.

Wolfson didn't stop there, however, and sought out another
opponent, Lubarski and worked out a plan to discredit us. On
Sunday there was a meeting with M. Katz from New York.
When it came time for questions, Lubarski got up, unrolled a
newspaper and dragged out the pair of shoes Wolfson had
bought. He started to give a speech about how we were
cheating the workers. What could we do or say? It hurt us
deeply: we were silent and we were frustrated.

As I already said, being unwilling or unable to realize that
the fate or our cooperative was already sealed with Bornstein's
act, we went on with our further attempts to grow, just as if
nothing had happened. We decided to buy the building on
South Fifth Street and readied a big demonstration. We were
carrying out a lot of agitation among various unions. The
bakers union members made themselves special costumes, and
a very impressive march was led by Joseph Barondess, riding
on a white horse (which didn't want to walk): a sort of
prophesying of the future cooperative movement. The route
was a mile long and 1500 workers marched with dozens of

slogans.[70] Our cooperative store was decorated in red; many
fired revolvers in the air during the march. The march lasted
for hours. After marching through the streets, we marched over
to Musical Fund Hall at Eighth and Locust. We had prepared
special envelopes, and put them out on the seats. Barondess,
Moshe Katz, Louis Miller and I spoke. M. Gillis was the master
of ceremonies. We needed $800 to cover the expenses. We
counted the money we collected at the demonstration, and
there wasn't even enough to pay for the hall. A few weeks later
we began to prepare a big open house to dedicate the store.
Every evening, for five nights, we hosted a different union.
There was a speaker at each of the tables set up in the store.
The beer and schnapps with pastries didn't cost us anything.
Everything had been donated. The dedication was a great
success. We generated the money needed to cover the costs of
the demonstration march. That encouraged us anew and gave
us hope.

We decided that our cooperative should be incorporated,
that is, it should get a charter (a permit from the state). To
whom does one turn to apply for a charter? To a lawyer. Among
our ranks there was someone named Pokras, who was already
a qualified lawyer. We went to him. He explained to us that he
wouldn't make a profit off of our cooperative; it would only cost
$90 for the nominal expenses for the paperwork. We thought
with satisfaction: such an idealist, one of our kind, he really
doesn't want to exploit us; and we were delighted with Pokras.

A few days later I happened to be sitting in a restaurant. A
lawyer named Cohen was seated at the same table. I got to
talking with him about the cooperative and the charter which
we were planning to take out, and with great pride I told him
about Pokras' deal. He immediately became enraged. He
promised to get the charter for us for $40 instead of $90.

The situation with Pokras changed from great enthusiasm
to hatred. We decided to give Lawyer Cohen the job of taking
out a charter for $40. But this wasn't so easy for us to
accomplish. Pokras and his family, which consisted of
Dubinsky, Hinden and Layenis, decided to take revenge on us

and destroy the cooperative store. And they didn't have to wait long to satisfy their thirst for revenge.

A short while after taking out a charter for our cooperative store, the following event came to pass. Five laborers came to the Philadelphia bakers union and explained that since they had been thrown out of their workplaces for being union members, and they were unemployed, they were appealing to the union to do something for them. After some discussion it was decided to open a cooperative bakery. I suggested that we issue 25 cent stamps. With these stamps one would be able to buy bread when the store opened. My suggestion was adopted and we swiftly printed up stamps for this purpose. But the stamps didn't sell as expected, so I was sent to New York to visit the unions and the united Jewish trade groups, and appeal to them for help.

The first union I went to in New York was the bakers union. They immediately voted to send $50. Unfortunately, they forgot about their decision and never sent a penny. I did manage to bring back $200 to Philadelphia. We had already had a sum of $600, so now we had $800 all together, instead of the necessary $1000. We decided to open the bakery with the money we had in hand. Then the search began for a suitable manager. Since we couldn't find such a person right away, I was urged to take on the position. Against my will, I agreed. I held the position for a couple of weeks. The cooperative bakery was losing $25 a week. Gersten became manager after me.[71] During his tenure, the bakery lost even more each week; and after him, Comrade Menkin became manager. It didn't go any better for him. The upshot was that before long, nothing remained from the entire capital. I was again approached about becoming the manager.

The cooperative bakery started to reduce its losses. But other problems and difficulties surfaced. All of the unemployed bakers expected to work at the cooperative bakery, which was impossible. As a result, discontent was generated in the bakers union. Then I received a directive from the union to take orders for bread from stores which didn't take union bread. That caused a lot of aggravation. Instead of running the bakery, I had to run around all parts of the city to get new customers. That was only half of the problem. Our delivery of the baked goods was limited, so the bread used to arrive too late, and more and more was returned to us. The returned bread was as good as worthless for the general population, which wanted only hot and fresh bread, although that is unhealthy.

Our workers in the cooperative bakery didn't understand that one must apply oneself to the job conscientiously, although workers were also somewhat lacking when working in an ordinary union shop with a boss. At that time the bakery was losing only $4 a week. I suggested to the board of directors that they should subsidize the bakery with $2 a week, and we, the eight bakery workers, would also contribute $2 a week to cover the shortfall, each according to his earnings, even if only a few cents. The workers promptly refused to participate. Their complaint was very typical, suggestive of the crew with which we managed to make such experiments. "What do you mean we should give out of our wages? Whatever boss we work for pays us full wages; nothing is deducted!"

Well, what could the outcome of the cooperative movement have been other than failure? And thus, the bakery closed down even before our main cooperative, the shoe store, went out of business. After giving up the bakery, the woman from whose husband we bought flour came crying that we had ruined her. We owed them $25 for flour. We decided to transfer everything to her husband's name. When I was ready to go to Margolin, the lawyer, to transfer everything, it turned out that everything we owned had been dispersed. The only thing we had left was a horse. Since not everyone knew where we kept him, I gave him back to Melman. The man from the stable, where we kept the horse, calculated that we still owed him eight dollars. He belonged, however, to the same political club as Pokras (who had already put his anarchist activity far behind him). The stable man sent us a bill for eight dollars. The bill was written on a postcard. Pokras, however, advised him to send us a bill for $52, and without the least self-respect Pokras did, in fact, bring me the bill personally. I showed him the postcard with its request to pay $8. He asked me to give

him the postcard until evening. In my naïveté it didn't occur to
me that Pokras had sunk to such a level of treachery. But it
turned out that I never saw the postcard again. He claimed
that the postcard "disappeared." We refused to pay the $52
which we didn't owe. Pokras carried out his long-planned
revenge for not giving him the $90 (rather than $40) for taking
out the charter. He filed charges against the cooperative shoe
and hat store and brought us to court.

At the opening of the trial, Pokras pointed to us, the
defendants, and dramatically cried out, "They are all
anarchists." Then he proceeded to try and prove that the
cooperative shoe and hat store and the cooperative bakery were
one and the same. And his evidence on that score was
magnificent. Since we had used the words "workers
cooperative," and the bakers also used the words "cooperative
workers bakery," therefore they must be one and the same.
That just happened to be false; the bakery was actually a
branch of the bakers union and it had no business relationship
with the shoe and hat cooperative. The end result was that
even a capitalist court didn't want to help Pokras take his
bloody revenge on his former comrades. Pokras lost the case.

A Jew by the name of London came to America. He told us
that he was a baker foreman and that he knew Winchevsky
and Feigenbaum, and that he had even slept together with
them. He asked us to give him a job, at least for a short while.
We gave him work. He promptly slipped and fell on a rusty
nail. He wife came running right away screaming and crying,
"Well, Weinberg, my husband has been crippled by your
cooperative bakery. What should I do? Where can I get money
for rent and food!?"

We had four rooms on South Street, over the shoe store, and
we decided to rent the place to London's family for 12 dollars a
month, and to open, just for his sake, a bread store, so he could
make a living. After four months he owed us $50 for bread and
he hadn't paid any rent the whole time. Aside from the fact
that London hadn't paid, the other tenants followed his
example and didn't pay either. Sending Margolin[72] the lawyer
to collect had no effect and my going to them personally was

also futile. The tragicomedy of London's case was the final straw. Passover was coming and he came to a meeting of the board of directors insisting that, since Passover was coming, his wife would like us to repaint the rooms for the holiday. The board of directors were understandably quite peeved and we answered her: since you haven't been paying for bread and rent anyway, you could at least do the painting yourselves. And London was not the sort of Jew who lacks an answer. "I could get a rabbi to give a ruling on this question."

A shirt makers' strike was going on in Philadelphia. The strike was bitter and protracted. Strikers were going hungry. I came to a meeting of the board of directors and appealed to them: since our store is now losing money, let's take $25 out of our own pockets and bring it over to the strikers, and the money will be given in the name of the cooperative store.

I brought the $25 to a meeting of the strikers, and addressed them. "In our city there are hundreds, thousands of stores; have you ever seen any one of those storekeeper lift a finger on your behalf? Did any of them, even a single one, support you in even the smallest way? But one store is an exception. There is a store on South Street, founded by workers, managed by workers for the interests of the workers. If each of you workers in Philadelphia would support the store, as you support, through your purchases, every other non-worker-owned store in Philadelphia, then I would be standing in front of you with a check for $1000. And further: if all of the workers would realize the importance of the cooperative movement, I am sure that you wouldn't even have to go on strike at all. Certainly, you would not be lacking food and clothing. Cooperative stores would lend to all of you who are needy. You, the workers, have not yet proved that you comprehend how vital the cooperative movement is in your interests. Because of this, our existing cooperative store is poor and I can only bring you the insignificant sum of $25 as a contribution to your strike."

The strikers boisterously applauded my speech. Well, we expected that the excitement and enthusiasm that our act would bring out among the workers in Philadelphia would bring us more proceeds the following week. Our hope was not fulfilled. They avoided the store even more. We put out a brochure written by Dr. Barbour.[73] We distributed the brochure in the letter-boxes. We printed and distributed thousands of leaflets, called meetings, but it didn't bring any improvement in our store's business. One of the final attempts to save the store from going under was: turning to the unions. We suggested to them that everyone who showed a union booklet would receive a price reduction of 5% for his union. The English unions gave us a chilly reception. For them, this was an undertaking led by "foreigners." In truth, it was just that. Even the place where the store was located, was far from the American labor population. The Jewish unions, from whom we justifiably expected a warm response, also bitterly disappointed us. Typical was the remark of a pants maker when I came to their meeting. After my speech, he got up and said, "So you've come up with a new trick."

When I happened to run into workers, members of the cooperative, and I asked them, "Why don't you come to the meetings? Why don't you shop at our own cooperative store?"— I received the following answer: "I'm already getting old, and I must first think about practicality, and find a store for myself. So how can I keep supporting the cooperative movement when it strives to put all the storekeepers out of business?" How could I respond, given the sad truth, especially the condition of the Jewish workers? It hurt me, and though I am always talkative at the podium, I held my tongue. The great experiment of our first attempt of a cooperative movement among Jewish workers lasted four years. What lovely dreams we wove during the first months of the founding. What great hopes we built for the future! These were the finest moments of my activism in the labor movement. However, no matter how hard we struggled against its going under, with Bornstein's act which aroused distrust among the members, the cooperative movement was already doomed to failure. When the end came I, who had never shed a tear as an adult, bawled like a small child.

The dream of the future society, where workers would be equally producers and consumers, was declared bankrupt after four years of struggling for its existence. The store went bankrupt and nothing was left of it. Although the workers didn't understand the importance of the great experiment, and didn't show enough class consciousness, my eyes still become tearful when I recall the wonderful moments, the period of the existence of the cooperative shoe and hat store in Philadelphia.

Chapter 6

At the same time when we were reestablishing the *Fraye Arbeter Shtime*, the Jewish anarchists decided, at a New York convention, that in order to start a new newspaper it would be necessary to send out an agitator to establish groups and thereby lay the groundwork for an anarchist press. They were looking for a single man who could devote about three months for the planned tour and the lot fell to me. It was decided that I would be paid the same salary I was earning in the shop: $10 a week. The two treasurers, Michael Cohn[74] and B. Saffir, were supposed to pay me the salary. I traveled around for four months without receiving a penny. When I returned, the two treasurers handed me $10. I told them that they might as well keep it for the movement, and I took nothing. This had to be in 1898-1899.

The first stop on my propaganda tour was Pittsburgh. I had the address of Comrade Harry Gordon so I traveled to his house.[75] Opening the door, I saw a table covered with a white cloth and laden with food, and everybody in the house was dressed in their finest. When those present caught sight of me, a diminutive man, lame in one foot, with a torn jacket, overcoat and umbrella, and with a very unattractive hat, everybody ran from the room and left me standing alone. It dawned on me that the guest, and especially his appearance, were a bitter disappointment for them. I stood alone in the center of the room and waited. Finally, Comrade Gordon took courage, opened the door and came in. After him, came Comrade Kisliuk.[76] I asked them why they had run away.

They didn't answer me. I understood all too well, however, that they had expected a large, tall fellow; in appearance, at least, like Jacob Gordin—with a large beard and a cane, well-dressed.[77] I continued, 'Are you embarrassed by my clothing, my luggage, or my hat?' No response. Thus, disappointed and almost angry at my appearance, they led me into the hall. The first lecture was so successful that I spoke twice more in Pittsburgh. And for many years after that, the comrades in

Pittsburgh remembered, not my appearance, but rather their embarrassment at the reception they had given me at the first stop on my first propaganda tour. Arriving in Buffalo from Pittsburgh, I looked up Comrade Zallen. I came into his store and he greeted me, as he would any customer in English, "Do you wish something?"

"Yeah," I answered, "I want to see you."

He finally figured out who I was and he asked me if I really was the very same Weinberg. He brought me into his room and welcomed me with tea. From what he said, I gathered that he had just married a really pretty girl. I also deduced that he was too embarrassed by my appearance to introduce me to her, and consequently, he sent me over to Comrade Perlman as soon as he could. First, however, he ran over there himself to forewarn them so they wouldn't laugh at me as they had in Pittsburgh.

At Perlman's house, there were two sisters who had just arrived, greenhorns. As soon as I walked in, they took one look at me, with my garments, hat and shoes, with my luggage and general shabby appearance, and they began to choke with laughter. I was starting to get used to it. Unfortunately, as I found out too late, my tie was also not properly positioned and that made me appear even more outlandish. Perlman brought me to the lecture. The two greenhorn sisters were ashamed to go with me, so they followed after us. At the door stood a fellow with a plate, and whoever was so inclined contributed something on the way out. Someone told me that a man came by and put in a whole dollar (at that time a dollar was equal to $10 today), commenting that he would be delighted give another dollar if I would continue speaking all night.

After the lecture, which was as well-received as it had been in Pittsburgh, the two greenhorn sisters were no longer ashamed of me. They brought me home, treating me as etiquette would require one would treat a gentleman. In Buffalo, I also spoke three times. Each time, more people attended. At the three lectures, just as in Pittsburgh, almost all the questions and discussions revolved around the eternal dilemma about the bridge (which means, in effect, common sense). What do you do when the majority want a bridge, and the minority don't want a bridge?

From Buffalo, I arrived in Chicago at six o'clock in the morning. The only address I had was for Comrade Levitsky, who had a cigar store (A few years later he committed suicide).[78] After I woke him up, Comrade Hursen came by and brought me directly over to the Edelstadt family, whose residence was the main guest house for all the visiting comrades. Upon Sarah Edelstadt's arrival, my appearance elicited the same reaction as it had in Pittsburgh and Buffalo. Sarah, too, ran from the room, choking with laughter. My moral victory was the only thing that saved my prestige on each occasion. Here, as well, we had a great success, even greater than in Pittsburgh or Buffalo. The first two weeks, I spoke seven or eight times.

May Day fell during my few weeks in Chicago. We found out that there was a large banner, stretching from one side of the street to the other in front of Rochester Hall, announcing that the great Abraham Cahan would be coming to speak on May First. That aroused in me the notion of revenge against the social democrats. Why? The reader will find out later. In Chicago I met up with Staller and Brenner, who just happened to be in town then. At a meeting that evening, the Chicago comrades decided to arrange an international gathering to be held at the same time as Abe Cahan's speech. The following speakers were invited: in Russian: Yitskhak Isaac ben Hirsh Tsvi HaLevy (Dr. Hourwich); in Polish: Graz Rubakovsky, an anarchist and an engineer, now very wealthy, living in America; in Yiddish: Brenner and I; a speaker in German and Lucy Parsons in English.

To say that our international May Day celebration was a triumph would be an understatement. The hall was filled by one o'clock in the afternoon and no more people were allowed in. The social democrats, with Abraham Cahan, had a spectacular failure. Their hall was as deserted as a cemetery. Abraham Cahan cursed the anarchists as much as he could and wanted. When Peter Zusman, the social democrat, met up with me, his first question was: why did you have to ruin our meeting? Couldn't you have arranged your celebration for the evening? As an answer, I told him about the following incident:

Comrade Bookbinder (recently deceased) was living in Providence, Rhode Island.[79] I received a letter from him telling me to come and give a lecture. They would reimburse me for the travel expenses. When I arrived in Providence (this was wintertime), I was informed that it was illegal to pass out handbills in the city; one could only paste them up. Comrade Bookbinder and another comrade trudged around a whole night in the cold, pasting up the announcements of my upcoming lecture. The following day, the social democrats in Providence saw the announcements and it so inflamed their democratic spirit that they went around the whole night and tore down the handbills. On the third day, we found out about the damage they had done, but it was already too late to do anything about it. We went to the hall feeling bitter and discouraged. A dozen people came. It was freezing cold because the hall owner had apparently figured that it wasn't worth heating the building. We decided to go to Bookbinder's house and cancel the public lecture. A comrade from Boston promptly offered $3 to help pay for the hall. However, we went home with Comrade Bookbinder and I gave my lecture over a glass of tea. This was the reason I was driven to retaliate against the social democrats in Chicago.

The first Yiddish anarchist poet was our beloved friend and comrade, David Edelstadt.[80] His family was very different from the usual families one encounters. All of them, the parents, the brothers and the sisters, were anarchists.

After David Edelstadt's death, his whole family was living in Chicago. Many of us in the Jewish anarchist movement had heard of Sarah Edelstadt, David Edelstadt's sister. One especially heard about her talent as a speaker. A party of young men went on an expedition to take a look at Sarah Edelstadt: Comrade Feldman from Boston, Comrade Telson from Philadelphia and I. Thanks to the propaganda tour, each of us arrived with hopes expecting to be the lucky man to become the life partner of Sarah Edelstadt. The lucky one turned out to be the second one to go to Chicago for that purpose: Comrade Telson.[81]

When I arrived in Chicago, I soon discovered why the Edelstadt house was the place where all the comrades in Chicago gathered. Coming to their house for the first time, I saw a long table with people dining. I assumed that our comrades were dining at the Edelstadt's guest house as one would eat in a restaurant. It didn't take long for me to find out that I was mistaken. None of the diners paid a penny. Both Edelstadt brothers, Abrasha and Aaron, paid for the upkeep of the house. This was especially the case with Abrasha, who was earning at that time five or six dollars a day. In addition, I learned that both brothers suffered from the proletarian disease. It deeply distressed me that people who had no idea what the word "work" even means, could misuse it in the worst way. I decided not to remain silent, and to see that the vile abuse by the "diners club" at the Edelstadts' place would be stopped. At the first opportunity, I talked it over with Sarah. I told her openly that to allow irresponsible parasitic people to eat off the toil of her two ailing brothers was senseless and also a great injustice. To this she agreed, and they decided to move, not only out of the house, but also so far away from the neighborhood where all the "diners" lived, that they literally could not come.

The Edelstadt family moved into a house near Lincoln Park. But the association of freeloaders didn't forget about their *gratis* guest house. Every Sunday, the troupe would march four or five hours from Halstead Street to Lincoln Park. Then they used to stay and eat two meals. But at least that was only once a week. And the good, dear Edelstadt comrades couldn't refuse to give the loafers the two free meals a week. In Chicago, I continued working at cigar making. I spent seven or eight months there. When I became unemployed and the prospects of getting another job were not favorable, I decided to leave Chicago.

Our martyrs of 1887 didn't sacrifice their lives for nothing: their murder at the hands of the state brought into our ranks the rare, gentle, deep-thinking and sensitive soul that was Comrade Voltairine de Cleyre. As is now widely known, the anarchist movement in America and worldwide attracted dozens of new members into its ranks as a result of the martyrdom of our five comrades. (I myself, in fact, became interested in the anarchist movement while reading their speeches.) Who knows if the repeat of the state murder in 1927, the legal murder of our martyrs Nicola Sacco and Bartolomeo Vanzetti won't also bring in new recruits to our ranks.

There must still be, here and there, a number of people whose souls are not entirely preoccupied with trivialities and pursuit of their careers! Time will tell, sooner or later, if my hope is justified or not.

From Chicago, I returned to Philadelphia. There I found that several changes had taken place. The second anarchist group, The New Generation, had dissolved. Only the original anarchist group, the Knights of Liberty, remained. The group had also decided to give up the Yom Kippur balls. Comrade Voltairine de Cleyre found herself at that point in England, where she lectured in many cities to great acclaim.[82] The Jewish anarchist movement there was moribund; only the Arbeter Fraynt group remained. The Jewish anarchists approached de Cleyre, asking if they could get a speaker from America who could promote the Jewish anarchist movement in England. Her reply was that, for organizing Jewish unions and building an anarchist movement, there was only one—the Philadelphian Weinberg. Comrade de Cleyre's suggestion led to Comrade Baron's writing me a letter, inviting me to come and spend some time in England.[83]

At that time, I was the father of a two-year-old son.[84] Consequently, I made a request of the English comrades that they should send me a round trip ship ticket, as well as $10 a week to support the child. My conditions were accepted; they sent me a ship ticket and three weeks' wages for food. Arriving in London, I quickly learned that a bitter factional struggle was going on in the Jewish anarchist movement there. One faction was the "Baronists" and the other, the "Kaplanists."[85] The Baronists had brought me over. I had no idea of this, of course, until I arrived in England. The Kaplanists strongly resented the fact that the Baronists had managed to accomplish the feat of bringing a speaker all the way from America. So what should they do about it? Should they forget about their trivial quarrels and help make my visit a success? Nothing doing. Instead, the Kaplanists announced that, at the same time as I would be speaking in Christ Church, and moreover, in the same street, Comrade Kaplan would give a series of twelve lectures in Sugar Loaf Hall. The Baronist faction decided to set a price of three pennies for my lectures (six cents admission for each lecture.) So what did the Kaplanists do? They decided not to set a price at all, but to have free admission.

About a hundred people came to the first lecture. It seems that the London workers made a strike against me. It was a great pity: to come thousands of miles to speak before a mere hundred people. The Baronists were even more upset that I was, and Comrade Baron simply collapsed and couldn't go to work the next day. The Baronists then decided to lower the admission price to two pennies. The result was—they started coming by the hundreds. The Baronists got even more encouraged and lowered the price to one penny, and the hall, which could hold 600 people, became too small.

The Kaplanists had a terrible flop. At the first one-penny lecture, a man came up to me and introduced himself, "I am the self same Kaplan, and I gave up my lectures in order not to interfere with yours." I spoke twelve times in London, with great success.

Aside from London, I also spoke in Leeds, Glasgow and Liverpool. The most interesting event occurred in Liverpool. There, a dispute broke out over who would be the moderator. There were two contestants for the honor: Comrade Livay and Comrade Jaeger.[86] Comrade Jaeger was a big boaster. I remember how he told me proudly and solemnly how he had debated August Bebel and beat him. For him, it was not enough to have debated Bebel, which was a pretty fantastic deed in and of itself. Unfortunately, both comrades, Jaeger and Livay, lived in the same house. They fought for a long time, until it was decided that Comrade Jaeger would be the moderator.

Fate determined, as it turns out, that Comrade Jaeger would not serve as moderator after all. Being certain that he was the moderator, he stood outside talking. Comrade Livay, meanwhile, took advantage of the chance opportunity of Jaeger's lateness and stepped in as moderator. I don't know to this day if I would have come off as badly with Jaeger as moderator, as I did with Comrade Livay. One thing, however, is certain. I had never before had such a moderator. Comrade Livay opened the meeting and started talking. Five minutes passed and he was still talking. The first half hour thus elapsed and Comrade Livay spoke so fervently and unhurriedly, that it didn't occur to him to stop himself and let me speak. Gradually, mutterings and exclamations began to be heard: Where is the speaker from America? And Comrade Livay answered, "You don't have any patience. Okay, I'll stop right now." So I finally got the floor. While I was talking, Comrade Jaeger came in. Seeing what Comrade Livay had done to him, he became upset and ran out of the hall without hearing my lecture. Coming home (I was staying at their house), we had a new surprise: the door was locked and bolted from inside. We knocked and knocked, but Comrade Jaeger didn't want to let us in. It was raining outside and we started getting wet. Fifteen minutes went by; a policeman came along and asked us what the trouble was. We told him that we are knocking but it seems that no one can hear us. The policeman didn't hesitate and went to the door and started knocking with his club. Comrade Jaeger's wife promptly appeared and opened the door for us. Comrade Jaeger vented his anger on Comrade Livay shouting, "Crazy!" Both comrades, Livay and Jaeger, were the co-publishers of a local anarchist newspaper which had the strange name *The Mirror*.

The quarreling of the comrades in London grieved me deeply, and immediately after my arrival in the country I had made an attempt to bring together the Kaplanists and the Baronists. Comrade A. Frumkin[87] warned me that nothing would come of my attempt. And, as it later turned out, he was right; they went away from the peace meeting even more quarrelsome than before. The struggle revolved around the matter of who should be the leader: Comrade Baron or Comrade Kaplan.

When it came to the question of paying me, so I could return to America, it turned out that not a penny remained from the first twelve meetings in London; Comrade Baron had mortgaged everything worth anything. Luckily, I had $25 from America with me. The principal financial help for my return to America was from the provinces. Returning to London, a farewell gathering was arranged for me.

Peter Kropotkin[88] sent a letter of regret for not being able to come and wishing success. John Turner,[89] who was at that time very active in the English labor movement, also sent a letter of regret for not being able to come, and Comrade Cherkezov,[90] who was also invited, didn't come. The hall was overflowing. I came with my luggage because my ship was leaving at midnight, and I would have to go from the meeting directly to the ship.

Before the end of the meeting, a man stood up and read aloud a resolution adopted by the United Workers Society of London: Whereas they are really in need of a person who can help them organize the workers in London, and whereas I am the most suitable person for the job, they have decided to propose to me that I remain there for an indeterminate period. I answered that it really pains me but certain personal family duties make it impossible for me to accept the invitation. By then it was almost too late for me to run and catch the ship I was supposed to take—particularly as my luggage had disappeared. Well, I ended up remaining a Londoner for another few days, until the next ship was leaving for America.

Chapter 7

My friendship with Comrade Voltairine de Cleyre was very close. I often got the chance to hear her reading her lectures. She seldom gave a speech without already having written it down. There was a kind of holiness and love in her relations with everyone and especially with anyone who was working in the movement. It is entirely possible that she brought this spirit with her from the Catholic monastery where she had been a nun. We considered her to be the poetic soul of the anarchist movement in Philadelphia. She devoted herself to teaching English. All of our comrades learned the English language with Voltairine's help.[91]

Comrade Helcher was also one of those who studied English with her.[92] But this time the deep devotion and love, which she used to show each student, cost her dearly. Comrade Helcher became convinced that Comrade de Cleyre was in love with him. He had previously worked in the same shop with her. Comrade Navro, whom de Cleyre really loved, and with whom she had lived for many years, also worked there. When Comrade Helcher found out about that, it simply caused him to lose self-control. The remarkable thing is that Helcher never said or wrote a word to Comrade Voltairine about his love for her. How he could have thought that Voltairine was in love with him remains a mystery to me.[93]

After finding out about Comrade Navro, Comrade Helcher went and rented a room across from Comrade Voltairine's at Eighth and Fairmount. It didn't take long for him to act. Just a few days later he went out to the street and stood waiting for Voltairine at the streetcar stop. When Comrade Voltairine got off the streetcar, he confronted her. Without saying a word, he took out a revolver and fired at her. Before carrying out his deed, he had pasted on a mustache, and after firing, he tore it off. When Voltairine saw him and recognized who had shot her, she cried out, "You killed me?"[94]

Comrade Voltairine was immediately taken to the hospital, where she remained for five weeks. The bullet which hit her was lodged near the heart.[95]

As soon as Comrade Voltairine got out of the hospital after the five weeks, she started working to help free Comrade Helcher, who had been arrested. She went around taking up collections and did any other work that was required. The letter of the law, however, had its claims, especially when it came to a worker. The law of the state took a mentally ill person and brought him to trial, demanding punishment. Voltairine disappointed all the guardians of the law who were present, as well as the whole public opinion in America, with her refusal to testify against Comrade Helcher. Comrade Voltairine de Cleyre's anarchistic act, which most clearly revealed the amazingly beautiful, loving soul which was deeply hidden away within her, couldn't stop the revenge demanded by the guardians of the state. However, they didn't get everything they anticipated, either. Instead of sending him to prison, he was sent away to an insane asylum.[96]

But our Comrade Voltairine de Cleyre and Comrade Helcher's mother didn't rest. They applied all their powers to get him released from the asylum. They were able to accomplish this, too. Unfortunately, their victory was hollow. As it turned out, his own act affected him more terribly. Right after his release, he became even more wild, and his own mother had to consent to his being returned to the insane asylum. Comrade Helcher suffered several more years and then died.

I personally knew Comrade Helcher rather well before the tragedy. A number of incidents I know of confirm that something was odd about him, just as it is known, I believe, the underlying cause of his abnormality. Right after I first made his acquaintance, I found out that he carried a sandwich in his pocket wherever he went. Later, he came to me to find out the address of John Wanamaker (the late, wealthy department store owner).[97] I asked him why he wanted to know, and he explained to me that, as soon as he found out where Wanamaker lived, he would replicate the keys to the house, sneak in at night and cut his daughters' hair. Another time, Comrade Helcher said to me, "Remember, we were in Washington Park, and there was a woman (Vera Bayer) sitting at a table who looked like a mulatto? I'm in love with her! Her every expression is so sweet and pleasant. Weinberg, have you ever been to the Allegheny Mountains? There, in the Allegheny Mountains, I'll pick out the tallest mountain, and on the peak, I'll build a castle for me and her." He asked me for the woman's address, and I told him to write to the *Fraye Arbeter Shtime*, because she was also an anarchist.

I mention these few incidents that throw an entirely different light on his deed against Comrade Voltairine de Cleyre that also led to the ruin of his own life. Recalling these, I will permit myself to say that this case, and other such cases I will touch upon, have convinced me that the basic motive was sexual dissatisfaction, let alone the absence of love and whether one wants it or not. Who is more responsible for this condition, if not the entire unnatural system on which the present capitalist scheme maintains itself?

Speaking of Comrade Helcher, I must also stress that this wasn't the only occurrence of this sort of tragedy for which we may hold the present society responsible. I recall, now, the terrible way which Comrade Cohen ended his life. In a condition of insanity, he first poisoned himself, then cut his throat, and finally burned himself to ashes.[98]

A second tragic case was Comrade Lukhovsky, who had a family. One day, he went off to Fairmount Park and cut his throat. By other means, but just as tragically, Comrades Sherman, Rosenthal, Seltzer and Zalkin also took their own lives. And one must remember that we are only talking of the comrades in one city, Philadelphia. Who can calculate the huge toll of victims that we, the enslaved, pay year in and year out in every part of the world?

I must once again return to Comrade Voltairine de Cleyre. There was an entirely different tragedy with her. She neglected family life because of the great interest and devotion to our anarchist movement and ideal. For example, Comrade Voltairine de Cleyre went and learned to speak and write

Yiddish because she happened to work primarily with Jews and because she considered it very fortunate that we have a weekly publication, the *Fraye Arbeter Shtime*. Later, she translated I. L. Peretz's famous brief social essay "Fear and Hope" for the *Fraye Arbeter Shtime*.

I recall now an entirely different episode: Comrade Voltairine de Cleyre arose one morning cheerful and happy, washed herself and put on her best clothes; then she went to a photographer to have her picture taken. Whoever wants to see that unforgettably lovely smile has only to take a look at that picture. But how many such moments did our dear Comrade de Cleyre feel in her life? —very, very few.[99]

Our last encounter before her death was in Chicago. She was the type of person who had to stay active. She was cheerful, joyous, and full of enthusiasm, working for the Mexican revolutionary movement, led by the two brothers Enrique and Ricardo Flores Magon through their weekly Spanish publication *La Regeneración* in Los Angeles. One side of the paper was edited and written by Comrade William C. Owen, the 85-year-old veteran of English and American anarchism, who died in London in 1929.[100]

Comrade Voltairine de Cleyre called me to a meeting, one of many she used to call for this purpose. She made a lengthy discourse about the anarchist spirit which was widespread among the peons (Mexican peasants). She was certain that the propaganda from the Magon brothers would eventually bring about an anarchist revolution by the peons in Mexico. I don't know why, but the whole movement never had the attraction for me that it had for Comrade Voltairine de Cleyre. In any case, that was the last activity to which she sincerely devoted herself. That was the last time I saw her. Today, her grave is located near the place of our unforgettable martyrs in Chicago, in Waldheim Cemetery.[101]

After Voltairine de Cleyre comes, naturally, George Brown; this simple, always-smiling comrade, was just as tightly linked with our movement as Comrade Voltairine de Cleyre. I was very close friends with him, too. A characteristic trait of Comrade Brown was his simplicity. Once, he was invited to give a lecture before the Ethical Culture Society on the topic: "Anarchist Morals."[102] After the lecture, the questions began, and one question was addressed to Comrade Dr. Brown (in full seriousness). Our Comrade Brown answered with his smile, "You call me by the title Doctor, when the truth is that I have studied for years and years to become what I am today, a shoemaker."

His humor was always a sort of accompaniment to all that he had to say, on whatever topic. The Philadelphia government sometimes used to permit free speech at City Hall, and Comrade George Brown was usually the chief activist speaker. Once, I happened to hear a speech of his about Free Love, the most important parts of which still remain in my memory.

"People go around saying that we are bomb-throwers. Others say we don't believe in legal marriage, and I myself am accused of practicing this. I don't deny that last accusation. On the contrary, I will show you that it is true. And now to the story that I want to tell you:

"When I am not working, I like to go to a park. Seeing as the law allows me to choose which park I want, I usually choose the second most beautiful park in America, which is located in Philadelphia—Fairmount Park. And of course I always have a companion in the park, a book. Sitting, thus, one time on a bench in the park, reading a book, a girl came by and glanced at me. But how do I, a poor worker, presume to think about making the acquaintance of a girl? I sat until evening, and then took myself home. The next day I came and wanted to sit down in my usual place near the hill. I looked around and I immediately noticed the same girl who walked by me the day before; she was sitting under the same tree where I always sat. I approached and also sat down there. I glanced at the girl: she sat engrossed in a book. I became curious to know what she was reading. I asked her where she got books to read. She answered me—in the library. That an American girl should be reading the same books as I was really surprised me.

"Thus did I become friendly with this girl.

"One time the girl spoke up: 'Why do you always have to escort me home? Let me escort you.' That struck me like thunder. I lived at the time in a little room right in the tenderloin neighborhood. So, how could I permit her to come and find out where I lived? But having no other choice, I consented. At the house, I invited her to come up and drink a glass of tea and our acquaintance became more intimate. According to everyone, whether they call it God or nature, we sinned against whoever it was that created in us the desire to reproduce because it gives us pleasure. The law did not have the least connection with our becoming acquainted. Consequently, it would have been pointless to go and get from the law a paper to permit us to live in the same room and to love each other. Poor as we both were, living from our own labor, we did the best we could: we ate together, lived together, and the result was two children. Now we are busy with the upbringing and educating of the two children. We don't hate each other; we have differences of opinion. Our families are unhappy with our way of living, mainly because we haven't gone through the ceremony of getting permission for it from the city and the church. What is most important for us is that the children should grow up in such a spirit that religion and law should remain for them a dead, unknown phenomenon.

"This, my friends, is the terrible free love in which we anarchists believe.

"What will happen if we grow tired of each other? We'll part. We will, however, both bear full responsibility for the children which we brought into the world.

"And another thing: I want to tell you a secret. The girl about whom I just told you, is among you, the audience. You see her every Sunday selling literature and passing out handbills in connection with our work. This is Mary Hansen."

And his speech, which was as always interlaced with his broad humor, elicited public comments from the audience:" He's goddamn right!" Even one of the detectives called out, "He's a smart man."

Now sixteen years have already passed, and Comrade Brown is no longer among the living. His dead body was cremated.[103] Comrade Mary Hansen has remained in the anarchist movement. She has also developed into a gifted poetess.[104]

Comrade Gordon became acquainted with Voltairine de Cleyre, with whom he took English lessons, and after that also with George Brown. Comrade Gordon gradually drew both of them into the circle of the Jewish anarchist movement, and they used to come often to give us English lessons. In those days, freedom of speech was more or less a fact, and for many years both tirelessly led public English propaganda meetings every Sunday evening at City Hall. That lasted until 1907, when the great crisis broke out in America.[105]

In Philadelphia alone, there were 100,000 unemployed. The times were terrible. At a meeting held in Kensington, it was decided to call an international meeting where we would demand jobs for the unemployed.[106] The international meeting was held in New Auditorium Hall, Third and Fitzwater Streets. Brown and Voltairine spoke in English; speakers from New York spoke in Italian.[107] Without my knowledge, it was announced that I would be the speaker in Yiddish. At that time, I held the position of organizer among the bakers. When a committee came asking me to address the meeting, I went immediately.

As soon as I had begun to speak, before the packed audience of mostly Italians, people began to shout that I should stop talking. The moderator, Comrade Finkler, appealed that they should hear me out. I tried once again to begin my speech, but to no avail. Then Voltairine de Cleyre read her speech. The meeting ended with a call to march on City Hall demanding work, and the audience began heading for the doors.[108]

The police of our city, the city which is famous, more in jest than in seriousness, as the city of brotherly love, were exceptional in their brutality. When they received word of the march that was to take place (via their spies at the meeting, of course), they readied themselves and converged on City Hall from all parts of the city. As soon as the hundreds of Italians showed up on Broad Street at City Hall, the police fell upon them with clubs. Heads were split left and right; workers' blood spilled in rivers on Philadelphia's main street. It was an ironic-tragic twist on the famous saying that gold is lying around on the streets of America. Underfed workers from Italy had been given a taste of that gold. It was a blood bath from their own bodies; that was the way American justice satisfied their hungry, tired bodies.[109]

Furthermore, we found out that many of the Italians were arrested. We didn't yet know exactly who they were nor how many. In the evening, I found myself in the Colonial Café.[110] It was already twelve midnight when a detective showed up and arrested me. In the station house, I promptly discovered that all the cells were full with over fifty wounded Italians. The same day, Voltairine de Cleyre had been arrested and was being held for $1800 bail. Many Italian comrades were held for high bail amounts. I was held for $2,500 bail. We were all released on bail.[111]

Our trial began three months after our arrest. Five days before the start of the trial, the socialist lawyer Nelson let me know that he was refusing to defend me, but would defend Voltairine de Cleyre.[112] I went to see a well-known political lawyer Wessel. After hearing me out, he said to me, it's nothing, a bluff. And for $250, he would prove it in court.[113] It is also noteworthy that Sulzberger, the judge, was Jewish; Wolf, the district attorney, was Jewish; Gold, the detective who arrested me, was Jewish; I, the defendant, also Jewish.[114] The charge against all of us was: conspiracy against the state and incitement to riot.

Judge Sulzberger asked if there were witnesses to prove the charge. The district attorney said, no, he only had written testimony. And he got down to business. First, he read out a letter in which I was invited to come speak on the topic "Radical Literature" at a newly-founded progressive library in Rochester. A second letter was from the Peterson Library, to come speak to them on the topic, "The Exodus from Egypt.' The jury didn't understand what Exodus from Egypt signified, so Judge Sulzberger proceeded to explain it to them. The judge then proceeded to undo the charge and dismissed the case against me. Voltairine was also freed. Two Italian comrades got two years, one got a year and a half, and one got three and a half years. They were found guilty of firing at a policeman.[115]

I was immediately given an envelope with the belongings which had been taken from me during my arrest. Inside were a watch worth a dollar, and six cents. I still remember the look Judge Sulzberger gave first my wallet, and then me.

Two weeks after the trial, I took to my bed, with the same painful leg which was a perpetual reminder of the accident when I slipped and fell in London. To my great surprise, a bakery owner, Newman Beard, who always had an open shop, appeared before my bed. He explained that he didn't believe in "Yom Kippur" (making amends). He just came to see how I was; he had heard that I was ill.[116]

Gradually he began to tell me what had brought him to see me. "How much," he asked, "did you give the lawyer?" I told him, $250. "That was wasted money," he said. "Do you want to know who got you released? I did," he said, "Nobody else."

I didn't even begin to understand, so he undertook to explain it to me: "I know how much trouble you caused us, the bakery owners, with your union and cooperative bakery. You impoverished us. Well, six or seven of us got together a few months ago to discuss plans to get rid of you. Since one of my brother's sons, just over from England, is willing to do anything, so we thought, let's get him to swear out a warrant that he heard incitement to rebellion against the government... and he swore out the warrant.[117] When I came to my senses, my conscience started bothering me: what is this, making a frame-up of a blameless Jew? The case was, however, already at the district attorney. I ran to the other bosses and explained to them that Weinberg will get three years punishment; if we don't get the case out of the district attorney's hands, I'm going to expose the whole thing. They asked me, panic-stricken, so what should we do? I explained to them: I found out that it's too late to suppress the case; the trial has to take place. We have to take the chief witness and hide him for the duration of the trial. This will cost $200. And the chief detective took him away and hid him during the first days of the trial. This is what got you released, and not your lawyer!"[118]

After he left, the nurse found a five-dollar bill that he had slipped under the pillow. Also remarkable is the fact that this same Newman Beard still doesn't keep a union shop to this very day.

Chapter 8

It took place in 1906.[119] It was already a good few years after the demise of our first dream, the Cooperative Shoe and Hat Store. Many of us began to feel a yearning to do something. We began to talk among ourselves about forming a committee.

Several comrades came to me and suggested that the committee start by setting up a cooperative house. I explained to them that cheap rent is not the same as a commune. So what should we do? Although we were "-ists" (with various ideologies), we were all against exploitation; accordingly, I suggested that we enter into the house with the goal of saving a sufficient sum of money to be able to purchase a farm (land). There, on the land, we would be able to produce the necessary foodstuffs through the toil of our own hands.

My suggestion was accepted and we promptly proceeded to work on implementing the plan. We rented a nine-room house at Sixth and Jefferson Streets for $35 a month. Each person was obligated to bring in $10 a month.

The first difficulty was finding a radical woman who would cook and keep house. Finally, we managed to find such a woman: Comrade Mirl. When we started the house, we also had members from New York. A few of those in the cooperative house were the comrades: Geventer[120] and his girl Kerman, Axler, Y. Katz (Ketzenbaum), Broide, Yetta,[121] Weinman, myself, and others: all together twelve members.[122]

Every Sunday, a dollar was taken from each person's wages for expenses. The burden of the expenses was divided equally among everyone. When we had $350 in the bank, we began to discuss buying a farm. A fellow was found who wanted to sell us a farm for $8000, with a $2000 down payment. I was opposed to the idea, recalling the "estate" in Carmel. My main argument was: we have $350; how can we agree to pay a full $2000 now?

At that time, the famous Russian revolutionary Yekaterina Breshkovskaya arrived in America. She came to Philadelphia for two weeks. The Philadelphia "parlor radicals" rejoiced and were sure that she would stay with them.[123] We started to campaign that she should lodge with us in the cooperative house, because how could it possibly be otherwise?! And we did, indeed, win. She chose to be with us, the proletariat. You can imagine our jubilation.

Those remained two historic weeks of beautiful, lovely reminiscences! Night after night we got together. The "babushka" kept all of us on the edge of our seats with her enchanting recollections of her experiences in Russia. When she got tired, Dr. Chaim Zhitlovsky[124] sang revolutionary songs and he sang with such gusto that we tired him out singing just as the "babushka" got tired out telling her stories.

The house had already lasted eight months when the same issues which undermine every idealistic experiment began to arise: the incompetence of the people is revealed along with the real motives for which the majority join various movements.

For example: Comrade Geventer brought his girl with him. He had to send her to a sanitarium for consumptives; he found out that it would cost him less in the cooperative. Our radical cook was inspired by our radical ideology. Seeing as she was attractive enough to marry, a volunteer was found for her in our house. Unfortunately for us, it turned out that he had no intentions of marrying her, after all. Of course, the cook blamed the whole house, all of the members.

Getting the money in also proved difficult. I realized that the ideology of most of the communards, if we could call them that, was to retain the house because the rent was cheaper. I was not overly enthusiastic for that purpose. In the end, we gave up our plan to found a commune by means of establishing a cooperative house. We returned each person's share of the accumulated money. Another dream ended in a burst bubble with disappointment and pain.

Several years passed. Once again a desire was felt to pursue cooperative activity. A certain comrade Mrs. Levin arrived on the scene, who showed a strong willingness to work. Comrade Caplan wrote to us from Boston that he was willing to come with his wife, who could also be a cook. This was, of course, one of the most important things for us in maintaining a house.

We, the Philadelphians, went to look for a house. This time we rented a six-room house on Morse Street for $15 a month. The members were: Comrade Levin and his wife, Comrade Caplan and his wife, Comrade Zarember and I: six in all.

Everything was going along nicely; it was clean and tidy. I began to weave my dreams for the future. I thought, now that we are so few in number, our success is assured. But my joy was in vain, premature. Again, it was proven how each and every experiment is doomed when those with whom one shares a dining table do not share in the work to advance the intended goals for which the experiment is carried out. Furthermore, in many cases, certain individuals join for entirely different motives.

It didn't take long before it became clear that Comrade Caplan had come to Philadelphia with the aim of bringing his lover from New York into the cooperative house. A written war was going on between the lover and Caplan's wife. When Caplan's wife found out that the lover wanted to come, she immediately agreed to it. She openly declared, and Comrade Caplan knew about this, that she planned to throw carbolic acid in the lover's face. It didn't matter to her, she said, if she would get the electric chair.

She began to receive letters from the girl, saying that she was very ill. Comrade Caplan's wife insisted that he bring her to the cooperative house. She apologized and conceded that all the letters she had sent were foolish. Comrade Caplan wanted my advice about the new turn with his love affairs. I told him that I was terribly afraid that this was nothing more than a scheme of his wife's to bring his lover in order to better carry out her plan.

I just happened to be in New York at that time and I met with Comrade Caplan's lover. This was the aforementioned Vera Bayer, whom Comrade Helcher was so in love with. I advised her not to come under any circumstances. But it turns out that the most foolish thing that a person can do is to give advice on love matters. It seemed to me that she would heed my advice; that's what she told me, even thanking me for the warning. Suddenly, a telegram arrived one Saturday saying that she was coming the very same day. Comrade Caplan and Fannie, his wife, went to the train station to meet her. They kissed, that is, the two rivals: Vera Bayer and Fannie Caplan. On Sunday, our entire commune went to the park. We had a wonderful time. At that moment, it really appeared as if everything would be all right.

On Monday morning, we all went to work, leaving Fannie and Vera in the house. Truth be told, everything was going too well and cordially. I felt that sooner or later something would happen. And it came a lot sooner than I thought.

First, Fannie made an attempt at poisoning Vera by putting poison in a glass of seltzer. When that didn't succeed, she poured a cup of hot fat she had readied on Vera while passing a glass of coffee. Vera was immediately taken to Hahnemann Hospital.[125] Wanting to avoid the involvement of the law, and fearful of public opinion, we presented it as an accident: she scalded herself through carelessness.

Vera Bayer was laid up in the hospital for six weeks. She had plenty of pains to endure. They cut pieces of skin from her body and patched her injured face. Thanks to the great skill of the doctors, when she left the hospital one could hardly tell that she had had such terrible facial injuries as we had seen that Monday when the horrible deed was done.

Fannie Caplan left for Boston with her children the day after her deed. After leaving the hospital, Vera Bayer went back to New York and took rooms with Comrade Caplan. I had thought that Caplan was one of our comrades whom fate had caused such a sad love-tragedy. The subsequent facts show that he hadn't earned the title "comrade". He abandoned the children and Fannie with no support whatsoever. He had a child with Vera Bayer, and later had the gall to claim that the child was not his, let alone taking any responsibility for supporting it. It didn't take long for us to receive new tidings: Caplan had already found a new victim: a greenhorn girl by the name of Comrade Flora, just arrived from London.[126]

Vera Bayer got together with a Spanish comrade and now she is no longer among the living. And I must further mention that Caplan is the same Caplan who years later spent a long time in prison together with the McNamara brothers on the charge of helping to blow up the most reactionary daily newspaper in America, the *Los Angeles Times*.[127] Caplan's love affair quickly brought an end to the second attempt at a communal house.

Chapter 9

The majority of the Jewish unions, as I previously mentioned, used to be what could at best be called seasonal unions. Every new season, there was a strike. After each season, barely any trace of a union remained. In 1909, I was an organizer for the Cloakmakers' Union in Philadelphia. The general secretary of the International Ladies' Garment Workers' Union at that time was J. Dyche. He sent me a letter telling me to come to New York and help reestablish the Cloakmakers' Union. I answered that I was willing to come, provided I was given money for expenses. Six weeks later, I finally received the money for that purpose.[128]

Arriving in New York, I showed up at the office of the Cloakmakers' Union, which is now known as the International Ladies' Garment Workers' Union. The office was then located at 25 Third Avenue, on the second floor in the back room. In the office were a broken table and chair, as well as an old safe. I was promptly told that there was so little money in the safe, that for months the secretary Dyche and the president Abraham Rosenberg hadn't received a penny in wages. And the same was true for rent and telephone. The only one who used to come to the rescue was Samuel Gompers, the president of the American Federation of Labor, who often sent in a check.

The more active members of the union at that time were: Polakoff,[129] Dyche,[130] Rosenberg, Mitchell, Kaplan, Kleinman, Wolf and Shore.[131] The first meeting was called, which I was supposed to address. In those days, a sheer terror regarding the bosses reigned in the garment industry. Workers were afraid to simply walk by the union office, let alone go inside. This environment was created by spying on the workers and making them fear for their measly jobs. The more faithful union people, the more class-conscious among them, used to bring their dues in the evening when spies couldn't as easily recognize them. Planting spies in the shop, outside and in the street, was the main weapon used by the cloak bosses to enslave the cloakmakers.

The meetings which we called were successful. Workers filled the halls each time. A few weeks after I got to New York, we managed to organize one of the largest shops, Slivik Brothers. The workers were used to negotiating with the bosses themselves; the union was just a seasonal scarecrow. On the third day after Slivik Brothers was organized, the following event occurred: A worker received a special job from the foreman, which had to be finished by one o'clock. At one o'clock, the foreman came by and found that the worker had not even started on the special job. The foreman asked him why. The worker answered, "Don't nag me!" When the boss came by later looking for the "special," he found out that it hadn't even been started on and he got angry. The worker didn't let the opportunity pass; knowing that it was in season and specifically in an official union shop, he answered him with some kind of a Russian curse. The boss didn't happen to understand any Russian, so he went right over to the bookkeeper for a translation. He became furious, of course, and ran back to the worker screaming, "Say it, say it again."

The worker didn't hesitate and repeated the curse. The boss gave him a swollen cheek. The worker came to the union office and met with me. I sent him to the union lawyer, Meyer London. At the same time, I called a meeting of the whole shop. At the meeting it was decided: punish the boss by not allowing him to appear in the shop for three months, and also require him to pay $15 a week to the worker for as long as he could not come to work. The meetings which we held were quite successful, but we couldn't, for the time being, attract the new members we needed to really build up a union. That is, by applauding ourselves, we couldn't in actuality establish a union. I became rather pessimistic and started going around to the editors of the Yiddish newspapers.

First, I went to see Comrade S. Yanovsky, the editor of the *Fraye Arbeter Shtime*,[132] and I asked him to write and to come speak to the cloakmakers. His answer was, "The cloakmakers are a bunch of nothings. You will accomplish more if you go on a lecture tour."

Then I went to Johann Polay, himself a socialist, and at that time the editor of *Yidishe Togblat*.[133] Having heard me out, he answered me very sharply that their paper doesn't go in for such things. I went up to see Louis Miller, the editor of the *Varhayt*. He heard me out and promised to do everything in the world, but not even a single word was published about the cloakmakers in the *Varhayt*. Lastly, I went to the *Forverts*. I invited Abe Cahan and B. Feigenbaum to come and speak. Cahan explained that he just gotten out of the hospital after an operation, but the pages of the *Forverts* would always be open to help organize the workers.

And the *Forverts* was, in fact, the only Yiddish newspaper that was open for us and for organizing workers in the Cloakmakers' Union.

The help of the *Forverts*, however, still didn't bring the thousands of cloakmakers into the union. I thought of a new plan: seeing as the Workmen's Circle had 20,000 members, and the majority of the members were located in New York, I figured there must be at least two thousand cloakmakers among them.

A committee consisting of Polakoff, Dyche and myself went to the executive board of the Workmen's Circle and I described the pitiful condition of the cloakmakers and of our union. I made it clear to them that it was their moral duty to help lay the foundations of a large and powerful cloakmakers' union. If they didn't do that, they would be indirectly supporting the perpetuation of scabbery: open shops. My concrete demand was that the Workmen's Circle should call a conference of all the Workmen's Circle branches in New York, at which plans for organizing the Cloakmakers' Union in New York would be formulated. The executive board of the Workmen's Circle agreed to my plan and promptly called a conference.

I went off to see Meyer London, asking him to help me and to come address the conference. The conference was a great triumph. Speakers included M. London, J. Dyche, and myself. The delegates swore that from now on every cloakmaker who was a member of the Workmen's Circle must also bring along a membership card from the Cloakmakers' Union.

As a result of the conference, it wasn't long before the Cloakmakers'Union picked up three thousand new members. Thus was laid the foundation for the later-renowned Cloakmakers' Union which successfully carried out the famous general strike in 1910. That strike led to the organization of the cloak and dressmakers into powerful unions, not only in New York, but also in all the industrial centers in America where those industries were found.

In the middle of the almost completely successful crowning achievement of helping to organize the Cloakmakers' Union, just when the plans for the general strike of 1910 were almost finalized, I became indisposed and had to take to my bed. When I became ill, a doctor was called: Dr. Bookman from Lebanon Hospital in New York.[134] He took two dollars for the examination, and smeared my foot. But a smear here and a daub there didn't help one bit. A thought occurred to me: we have our own doctors, after all. I called in the woman in whose house I was staying, and asked if she would be so kind as to telephone Dr. Hillel Solotaroff. [135] It didn't even take an hour before Comrade Dr. Solotaroff showed up, joking with me about everything in his own unique fashion. He started right in with me:

"Why did you crawl all the way up here? I can't catch my breath and I'll soon need a doctor myself. Why are you lying in bed? Your foot hurts and you call me? What do I know about foot ailments? Call a foot doctor. The only thing I was taught was how to deliver a baby. But since I'm already here, let me take a look. Does it hurt here? And not here? If it were an external wound, I would know," and he hummed a *gemore* tune.[136] "But it is possible that this is no more and no less than an attack of rheumatism. But the question remains, what kind of rheumatism is it? Does it hurt here? Then it's not rheumatism. So what is it then? It's entirely possible that it is a bone inflammation."

That's how he was talking, tugging his beard. "And it is also possible that it is tuberculosis in the bone... Does it hurt here? That means that with your help, I have actually figured it out. This indicates almost certainly that you suffer from tuberculosis. So Dr. Bookman is really a quack and the two dollars he took from you were wasted. What remains to be done now? Drag yourself over to Post-Graduate Hospital; there, they will take an x-ray of your foot, and then we will know for sure." After he had sung himself out and used up all his jokes about my ailment, he left.

The x-ray showed that our now-deceased comrade, Dr. Hillel Solotaroff, had actually correctly diagnosed my ailment. It was confirmed that I was suffering from tuberculosis in the joints. A famous surgeon, Dr. Albee,[137] operated on me and, of course, Dr. Solotaroff visited me often.

The operation was the second in the surgical history of America. The first took place in Denver. It was something extraordinary in those days to cure tuberculosis without cutting out the healthy portion of the joint along with the diseased portion. Rather, they only removed the unhealthy part, and filled it up with cement so that I wouldn't have to wear a brace. This Dr. Albee carried me around, lecturing the students about the great triumph which he had with me. When I got out of the hospital, I was transported to Philadelphia. Altogether, I spent about five months in bed. The cloakmakers affirmed their love and appreciation to me. They brought me the unexpectedly large assistance of $3000, a sum which helped me not only during my convalescence, but also later, to enable me to get by economically.

Many still remember that historic strike of the cloakmakers in Philadelphia, which lasted six months. In the middle of the strike, one of the pickets, Kaplan, was shot to death by a starving worker who had gone back to work during the strike. Kaplan's funeral was one of the most impressive demonstrations ever carried out by the Philadelphia workers.[138] Kaplan's murder gave more impetus and increased militancy among the genuinely starving strikers. Those of us who were following the strike closely became more and more certain that it would end up with a victory for the workers. I haven't the slightest doubt, even today, that the outcome of the strike would have been as we had anticipated, if there hadn't been two unexpected events.

The first and most important occurrence was that the bosses declared that they were willing to negotiate with a committee of strikers, but not with the settlement or strike committee of the union. Max Amdur was the strike leader at that time;[139] he wanted to show how powerful the union and the strike were, so that when the bosses wanted to meet with any committee whatsoever, the demands would stay the same as those the union had put on the table.

Amdur's handling of the matter was the biggest mistake that could have been made. It essentially sealed the doom of the strike. In reality, the bosses' stipulation was nothing more than a trick, (as it soon turned out.) When they heard that we gave in to their request, they understood that we were divided and weak. And when meeting with the committee of strikers, the bosses cruelly laughed at the committee's demands.

What the bosses did indicated that they were prepared to prolong the fight until they beat us. It would, perhaps, not have so easily succeeded if there hadn't, to our misfortune, just then broken out a struggle between the principal officials in the International Ladies Garment Workers' Union and Yitskhak Isaac Hourwich with Local #1. The financial ammunition which had helped us carry out the strike had come, until that point, from the Cloakmakers' Union in New York. The internal struggle in New York put a stop, in effect, to further possibilities of their supporting us financially.

It is difficult for me to describe what I lived through week in, week out, day in, day out, when I had to inspire the workers, saying that eventually victory must come; and now I had to be the one to go up and explain to the workers the situation I just described and concluded thus:

"Well, workers, the bosses beat us. They shouldn't think for one minute, however, that they have beaten us forever. Our ammunition ran out. Even today, at the same moment as we are giving up the fight which we carried out for six long months, we are making preparations for a new struggle! And though the cloak bosses are rejoicing, their joy will be in vain! As soon as the union possibly can, it will begin anew the rightful struggle for our demands." It was one of the most tragic moments in my life. Tears and cries choked the starving workers, the cloakmakers, in Arch Street Theater.

But my prophecy was more than fulfilled. The bosses laughed at the workers and further exploited and insulted them. The workers' anger grew so great that the Cloakmakers' Union felt the power to call together a mass meeting, not in Arch Street Theater this time, but in the largest hall we could get in the city: the Academy of Music. The hall was packed to overflowing.[140]   The workers' anger expressed itself in a unanimous firm decision to begin the fight anew by going out on a general strike. We had prepared and printed up appeals for the general strike. Everything was ready for the renewal of the fight. The bosses were no longer laughing. Public opinion mixed itself in and brought about a settlement. The bosses recognized the Cloakmakers' Union as a corporation with whom they must negotiate in their relations with the workers about the working conditions in their shops.

In Toronto, the Cloakmakers' Union had a lot of trouble during the process of founding an independent (IWW) union. In such a crisis, they usually sent for me. I came and gave a speech before the opposition, with the result being that they promptly all rejoined the American Federation of Labor. As soon as that happened, I was told to go back home. The pretext was that they needed an organizer who knew English. A second, similar incident took place during the cloakmakers strike in 1916, which lasted quite some time. When the strike was already in the fourth month and it appeared that the enthusiasm of the strikers might be waning, I also went around to many unions making appeals and collecting hundreds of dollars in support. After the strike, I was, as usual, politely told to "get along home."

And that reminds me of a lovely anecdote. Our former comrade S. Shore once stated publicly, "Comrade Weinberg reminds me of that horse you depend on whenever somebody has to be pulled out of the mud." Whenever it was tight in the union or bad during a strike, they sent for me, and then I was promptly forgotten.

Chapter 10

The pants makers were under the anarchist influence, as were almost all of the Jewish unions. Joffe, now a druggist, was a member. Moscowitz, now the president of the *khevre-kadishe*,[141] was also a member. Just at that point, Joe Margolin, a Marxist political refugee, arrived in Philadelphia from Siberia. The first task he took upon himself was to seize the unions for the political struggle. If a union were to decide that the political struggle is the only means, then, he thought (as did all or almost all Marxists), that the emancipation of the proletariat was assured.

Margolin didn't procrastinate and came to a union meeting to capture it for the political struggle. He was asked to show a union booklet. He didn't have one, of course. It turned out that he didn't even work in the trade. He was asked to leave the hall.

Margolin wasn't discouraged. He learned the trade and became a member of the union. Then he came to a meeting when few happened to be in attendance. He brought up anew the question of recognizing political action. He also wanted to know what I, not being a pants maker, was doing at the meeting. Most of the newcomers at the meeting recognized political action, by a majority vote. Margolin's enthusiasm is difficult to describe. For him, this was the greatest victory for socialism and the worst defeat for anarchism. Margolin was also an atheist. He used to get a wagon every Yom Kippur and travel around to all the synagogues.

Louis Miller was one of the initial founders of the *Forverts* and was also its first editor. Miller frequently came to Philadelphia to speak.[142] In my opinion, he gave the best speech on cooperation that I ever heard.

In Philadelphia, we were then in the middle of a long and bitter cloak maker strike over a boss named Blum (I have already told about that strike and the incidents of harassment.) The strike lasted six months, until we gave in. The strike leaders were Comrades Prenner and Staller.[143]

In those days, the social democrats bitterly hated the anarchists. Wherever there was an active labor movement, or a strike broke out, we, the anarchists, were the leaders. The social democrats were, understandably, irritated by that, and they used all sorts of means at every opportunity to discredit us in the eyes of the workers.

Two weeks after the strike defeat, I went to see Comrade Staller at his house. I looked in and saw Miller sitting there deep in conversation with Staller. I sat down and listened. Miller always took notes. As soon as Miller left the house, I asked Staller if he knew with whom he had been speaking. Staller answered that it was a reporter from the *Forverts*. I shouted out, "Do you know who that is? That is Louis Miller, the editor of the *Forverts!*"

We immediately felt that Miller didn't just coincidentally happen to come from New York disguised as a reporter from the *Forverts*. We thought up, down, and sideways and couldn't figure out the purpose of his action. But we didn't have to wait long to find out.

A headline ran the very next day which occupied almost the entire width of the front page, stating, "Philadelphia Cloak Makers Strike Sold Out By Two Anarchist Leaders!" You can imagine how we felt. Only social democrats could carry out such a piece of slanderous work. We replied with an article in the *Fraye Arbeter Shtime*.

As I already related, certain New York social democrats moved to Philadelphia to fight against the anarchist movement. As a matter of fact, Michael Zametkin was supposed to speak on the topic: "How much more freedom will the socialist society give over the capitalist?"—thus was written on the handbills in black and white. His lecture was arranged, of course, by the Philadelphia social democrats.

I had by chance come to the lecture to demand that they let me say a few words in favor of the union label on bread. Since I was given the platform before Zametkin's lecture, I introduced him. I remained seated on the platform to listen to the lecture, ignoring the rule that one speaker may not hear the next. It soon turned out that remaining on the platform was a terrible mistake on my part. Zametkin, giving me a fierce look through his thick glasses, began attacking the anarchist ideology. He entirely forgot about his topic, and I still remember the main content of Zametkin's attack.

First, the anarchist ideology is contrary to man's nature. Anarchism is in reality a utopia. Secondly, the present society cannot settle any question whatsoever except on the basis of a majority over a minority. "And imagine how absurdly this would work in reality: Philadelphia is in need of an Academy of Music; one must have carpenters, masons, porters, and others; instead of the porters, the carpenters come; no masons come, only porters; and so on, day in and day out; there is, after all, nothing to make them come. In an anarchist society, everyone can do what he wants, whatever he pleases.

"Or, take another example: I am a great fan of noodles. Now suppose we have an anarchist society. I go to one of their restaurants, wanting to eat noodles; there aren't any noodles; but I still want noodles. I am left wanting.

"Or a third case: it's raining outside, it's cold. I am sitting in my room reading a book when I remember that somewhere in a hall, a man is about to stand and give a lecture before the people; I close the book and go there, where the majority, the people, calls."

And Zametkin got excited, threw off his jacket and removed his collar, and started denouncing anarchism. Why anarchism is a senseless utopia, etc. He repeated his attacks again. When he finished, he sat down completely exhausted. The moderator let it be known that there would be an hour for questions and discussions. Since nobody got up to ask anything, the moderator wanted to close out the meeting. So I got up and asked for the floor.

I reread the handbill and asked everyone, "Did Zametkin speak about this or about a thousand other topics; not about the advertised topic, but rather, 'About Anarchism?' Well, I will have to defend anarchism. Zametkin kept coming back to the majority and the minority. But these are arguments which anyone belonging to a society will give you in any period. Is this appropriate for you, Friend Zametkin? Does right always lie with the majority. Let's take up world history. What is Galileo's and Copernicus' science and many other similar examples? Who was right, the minority or the majority? Was the truth really what the whole world believed?"

"Friend Zametkin is afraid that the Academy of Music could not be built in an anarchist society because one day there wouldn't be enough carpenters and another day porters would be lacking. What would Friend Zametkin do in a socialist society if the carpenters didn't want to come? He neglected to discuss that. We anarchists have such a thing as responsibility. If a person has understanding and respect, he will, with full responsibility, willingly carry out any work he has undertaken. If he doesn't have that, the "must" won't help, no matter how many laws you pass. Everyone knows that a soldier is a soldier and a prisoner does less work than a factory worker, despite the soldier and prisoner being more subject to the "must" than the factory worker.

"Coincidentally, it also happened to me that I was sitting and reading a book, Looking Backwards by Bellamy, but outside it was actually nice. I remembered suddenly, that Friend Zametkin was "speaking"... I didn't feel any call, however, but rather a keen desire to take a nap." The audience laughed heartily.

Zametkin rolled up his sleeves and started in with me. "If Weinberg had studied and understood something about the French Revolution, he wouldn't, with his fine mind and soul, be making a mockery. I am not saying that Kropotkin or Bakunin are crazy, but their ideas are crazy."

"It seems that with Zametkin," I remarked, "the ideas and the man are the same, and neither are clear." In his response, Zametkin lost it. He started mimicking my speech and also imitating how I limp on my lame foot.

On his way out after the "lecture," Zametkin came up to me and apologized, "It's no good when one gets excited," then we shook hands and went to a restaurant.

Almost the same thing happened on another occasion when William Edlin[144] came to Philadelphia to give a lecture on the topic, "The connection between Marx' doctrine and Darwinism."

And I was once again a committeeman at the meeting.[145] Edlin spoke for over an hour, giving the biographies of Marx and Darwin. He gave all kinds of details from their personal lives; he only forgot about one thing: their philosophy.

Of course, I didn't hesitate and, taking the floor, I made him aware that while the biographies are indeed very important, where was the scientific lecture about their philosophy that the handbill advertised? How did he expect to win over the audience this way?

I noticed that while I was speaking, Edlin leaned over to the moderator and inquired who I was. When it was time for the response, Edlin gave me a piece of his mind, scolding me, calling out pathetically, "Don't show a fool a half-finished job! To discuss the teachings of Marx and Darwin requires not one lecture, but minimum ten or twelve lectures." So who asked Edlin to undertake to address the whole topic in one lecture?

Often, writers and speakers try to answer the question: just what does the *Forverts* machine mean? Who is really the power behind the machine? One rarely receives a clear, satisfactory answer.

Fortuitously, I can answer the perennial question both satisfactorily and not satisfactorily. This may sound very strange, but, as you will find out, this is not far off the mark because of two incidents that happened to me. One incident was when I was pushed against the machine and didn't know who the machine was, or who was running it. In the second instance, I had the "luck" and the "honor" to be pushed directly against the machine, and against the power which drove the machine.

A good few decades ago, when Comrade Moyshe Katz was still in our movement, he really wanted the Workmen's Circle to send me out on a lecture tour. His claim was that, if acknowledged socialist speakers could be sent out, they could at least once send out an anarchist speaker. There are many acknowledged anarchists in the Workmen's Circle, so they could at least one time send a token anarchist speaker. Many comrades shared this opinion with Comrade Moyshe Katz. So Comrade Katz went and suggested it to the Workmen's Circle.

Nobody could deny the logical and fair arguments for it, and Katz suggested that they should send me on a lecture tour. But at the same time, the executive committee of Workmen's Circle answered, "No." That meant that they, the educational directors of Workmen's Circle, would not send out any anarchist speakers. Why? Where was fairness? Where was proportional representation?

Here, as you have probably guessed, I met up with the machine and couldn't respond, concretely with facts, who it was and who was behind it. However, that a machine existed in the Workmen's Circle and that it prevented me from being sent out on a lecture tour because I am an anarchist—this was clear for everyone.

Years later, when it became known that Max Pine was resigning as the almost perpetual secretary of the United Hebrew Trades, Comrade Sam Schor came running to me with a request that I run in Max Pine's place. I laughed, "All right, don't you know, Schor, that there is such a thing as the *Forverts*; would it allow me, an anarchist, to become the organizer of the United Hebrew Trades?"

Comrade Schor answered me, "The *Forverts* is dead. If you accept, you are elected!"

I consented. After that, I met with Saul Yanovsky and told him about it. And Yanovsky, in his typical fashion, remarked, "Tell Schor that he is an idiot. Abraham Cahan will never let you get elected."

I met with Comrade Schor, and he replied, "Tell Yanovsky that he doesn't know what he is talking about!" And Schor took out a handbill and wrote on a paper the name of each delegate who would vote for me and who would be opposed; and the holy guarantor of justice (and in most cases of injustice), her majesty, the majority, was on my side in black and white.

The struggle to see whether I would be the next secretary of the United Hebrew Trades flared up on the backstage battlefield, from which it became clear who the real machine was and who was running it.

Max Pine had a falling out with Cahan, the editor of the *Forverts*. At the time of his resignation, when Cahan found out about Schor's work, he immediately sent for Pine and made up with him. That, however, didn't help influence Pine to run again. He stuck with his resignation.

Seeing that it looked bad, Cahan sent for somebody named Isidore Cohen from the Forverts Association, asking him to run against me, in order to save the Jewish unions from anarchism. Isidore Cohen agreed to take on the holy mission.

The last days before the election were approaching and each delegate from the United Hebrew Trades was invited for a special consultation with Abraham Cahan. As we found out, Cahan repeated the same ultimatum to each delegate: "If you use your vote to elect Weinberg, the anarchist, you can say goodbye to the *Forverts*; its columns will be off limits to you."

Finally, the day of judgment arrived, election day, and remarkably, despite all of Abe Cahan's threats, the results were: 85 for Isidore Cohen and 79 for me.

That is, Abraham Cahan with his *Forverts* beat me, the anarchist, by a mere six votes. Long live the justice of the majority!

With that, the matter wasn't quite finished. The very same Isidore Cohen had written an article, a few months before his "election" as secretary of the United Hebrew Trades, which was full of accusations against many of the leaders of the Jewish unions. He had sent the article to the *Fraye Arbeter Shtime*. At that time, the district attorney of New York was carrying out an investigation into a bribery charge in the Jewish unions. Saul Yanovsky, the editor of the *Fraye Arbeter Shtime*, had, therefore, declined to print the article.

However, as soon as Isidore Cohen beat me, Yanovsky regretted Cahan's dealings and he came out with an editorial in the *Fraye Arbeter Shtime* the following week, demanding that Isidore Cohen withdraw as secretary of the United Hebrew Trades, or else he would publish the article. That worked, and Isidore Cohen immediately withdrew.

Abe Cahan then sent for Max Pine once again. This time, when it was already certain that I, the anarchist, would come out the victor in a new election, Cahan succeeded in getting his brother socialist, Pine, to budge. He agreed to continue as secretary of the United Hebrew Trades.

The *Forverts* machine with the power behind it: this was the very power which had triumphed over S. Schor and me.

Chapter 11

Morris Winchevsky

One time, in New York, I met Morris Winchevsky[146] on the Third Avenue El. Winchevsky asked me where I was living and where I was coming from. He was also coming from a meeting, from Sholem's Cafeteria. It wasn't long before Winchevsky was unburdening himself about the *Forverts*.

"The *Forverts*," Winchevsky told me, "did whatever it could to interfere and ruin the chance that I could serve the working class. However, it was absolutely not worth their while. Now I am a pencil pusher, working as an accountant in order to save the workers' money in Workmen's Circle and in the unions."

Winchevsky didn't know, or didn't want to know, that the good salary he was paid, as well as that of the many of his family members whom he had brought in to help him with the work, was thanks to the *Forverts*. The *Forverts* didn't do it out of love, but to quiet Winchevsky's opposition, and this was to some degree worth their while.

I had a second, not very pleasant, meeting with Winchevsky, unexpectedly, in a public school. A concert was being given in New York by the International Ladies' Garment Workers' Union. The office requested that I go and say a few words. I got to the location of the concert and found Winchevsky, whom the committee had invited for the same purpose.

Winchevsky, as a good social democrat, insisted that he be the closing speaker; that is, he would leave the last impression. I tried to discourage him from doing that, but he insisted on being the final speaker. As soon as I had finished speaking, the audience made for the doors. The moderator pleaded, "Don't go away; M. Winchevsky is with us and wants to speak." His effort was futile; the audience didn't think much of Winchevsky's speaking ability.

I knew this, and therefore I wanted to speak first. Walking home, I felt awful, and Winchevsky probably felt a lot worse than I.

Dr. Chaim Zhitlovsky

I already related how Dr. Chaim Zhitlovsky used to come every evening and sing revolutionary songs when the "Babushka" came to Philadelphia and stayed in our cooperative house. Dr. Zhitlovsky was immediately beloved by all of the workers, and even I was inspired by him. And when you like a person, you want to come in closer contact and work in a common enterprise with that person, and I had begun to work out wonderful plans for Dr. Chaim Zhitlovsky.

I decided that at the first opportunity (after his leaving Philadelphia for New York), I would meet with him and put my plans before him. I waited for him in a restaurant in the Lower East Side. I began to explain the plan to him, which I had put together as follows:

Dr. Zhitlovsky, here in America we have an extremely large force of Jewish workers. Their education is very limited; most of them are ignorant, never having had the chance to develop themselves. You, with your knowledge and abilities, could use all of it to help carry out the magnificent work that can just be imagined. The result of it would be the finest monument for you: helping the Jewish worker to progress so that he can think for himself. And I am certain that you, as a well-known revolutionary from Russia, will not refuse the task.

And Dr. Chaim Zhitlovsky answered me: "I am presently writing a book; as soon as I am finished, I will give you an answer." I am still waiting for Dr. Chaim Zhitlovsky's answer.

Yitskhak Isaac Hourwich[147]

Few of the activists in our Jewish radical movement showed such sincere friendliness in private life as Yitskhak Isaac Hourwich. Whoever met him personally soon grew to love him.

I remember the anger which his joining the International Ladies' Garment Workers' Union aroused among all the job holders in the union and especially at the *Forverts*—a person whom all knew and regarded as a sincere, honest person as well as a statistician. What, then, could have been his motive for joining the union, except to make a "housecleaning" there?

It is entirely possible that the union and *Forverts* politicians were right to be alarmed. And precisely these circles started in with him until they had driven him off, disregarding the fact that the largest local of the Cloakmakers' Union, Local 1, fought on his behalf until the bitter end.

A good joke comes to mind, indeed, in connection with that famous general strike of the cloak makers in 1916. How the settlement agreement was rejected because the word "full-fledged" appeared there, and how after the agreement was voted down, the workers turned around and accepted it as soon as the Yiddish gloss of the English word "full-fledged" was explained to them. Yitskhak Isaac sat down one time and gave an illustration of the above-described occurrence:

"Once upon a time, a pauper comes to a rabbi for advice. The pauper declares: I am, may you be spared, a very poor man—I and my whole family. We are crammed into one room; we are simply suffocating. What can we do?"

The rabbi replies, "Do you have, perhaps, a goat at home?"

"The poor man answers, 'Yes, Rabbi.'"

"So bring it into the house."

"The poor man doesn't know from farce. He goes home and takes the goat into the crowded room. He pays no heed to his wife's screams—it's no use, the rabbi ordered it! The pauper sees, however, that the situation has become a lot worse, so he returns to see the rabbi. Hearing him out, the rabbi asks him to go home and bring the cow into the house as well. So he goes and brings the cow inside. It's getting even worse; there really isn't any room to turn around. He goes back to the rabbi. This time, when he has already brought everything he owns into the house, the rabbi advises him to take everything back out again. After doing that, the poor man runs back to the rabbi and shouts, 'Dear Rabbi, it has never been so good as it is now, after taking the goat and the cow out of the house.'"

It was like that with the general strike and with the word "full-fledged," which the poor Jewish cloak makers hadn't understood because it was written in English.

When the Tsar in Russia convened the first duma (1906), Yitskhak Isaac immediately returned and came out as a candidate for the duma, and lost. After his return to America (where he remained the rest of his life), he held a debate with Emma Goldman about his reform activities which are today much praised on all the socialist, communist and even anarchist fronts.

A peculiar fate extended over his whole life and all his pursuits: he was a leader among the cloak makers, while he could never be a leader in the sense that a "leader" should lead a union. He was a civil servant, as a statistician, yet nobody could more sharply attack the state than could Yitskhak Isaac. He participated in Bryan's Populist People's Party, and also in T. Roosevelt's Bull Moose (liberalism) party. And yet, very few journalists criticized Bryan and Roosevelt as he did. He was an outspoken Marxist, but nobody criticized Marx as much as he did. He supported all kinds of reform parties, while he himself couldn't be a member of a party.

About Yitskhak Isaac Hourwich one can certainly say: he lived as a person whose ideas were socialist but whose soul was anarchist.

Chapter 12

Meyer London is another example of a social democrat that I, as an anarchist, really loved. I don't know what enchanted me more—his kind, animated speaking voice, or his personal magnetism.

In 1907, I had to go and speak in Ansonia, Connecticut, at a meeting to generate material aid for the revolution in Russia. I encountered Meyer London[148] on the train. It turned out that he was going to speak at the same meeting.

The chairman of the meeting was a former Republican state senator. I was asked to make the appeal for money. It brought in $300, although my appeal was, of course, in Yiddish. Judging by the audience's enthusiasm, moreover, the chairman also gave $10.

After the meeting, he asked Meyer London (who had spoken in English) who I was. London introduced me, and the chairman started up with me: "You are a wonderful speaker! If you had wanted, you could have gotten all those present to give you the shirts off their backs. And you are actually a cigar maker! That is really a shame! You know what? I have a plan for you, so you will never again have to work at making cigars. It is six weeks until the government elections; stay here with us in this city. You will only have to give a few speeches and your future is made."

I responded, "I could really use the money, but I don't believe in politics, that any political party whatsoever can bring any benefit or real help to the working class. The state, the government, is useless. I am for general rights of property, but not for private property; and as an anarchist, I would rather sit in a shop, earning with my own hands, than take you up on your offer."

The former Republican senator was surprised at first that I had turned down my good fortune. Then he appealed to Meyer London, suggesting that perhaps I didn't properly understand his proposal, and Meyer London responded:

"I have been trying for many years to make a social democrat of him, and I haven't succeeded; and you think you can succeed in making him a Republican? Your whole effort is wasted."

The politician with his golden offer was left standing there dumbstruck. The only remark that he still had the heart to make was, "You are very foolish to refuse my proposal for your future."

And thus, as you see, I passed up my golden opportunity.

Once, during my long association with the Philadelphia bakers union, I managed to be given a "golden" opportunity. The bakers union carried out strikes against five stubborn bosses. Among them were even Doctor Weinfield , "the priest" (as he used to be called) and a pastor. To defeat them more quickly, we decided to open a cooperative bakery near Weinfield's bakery, and this turned out to be three doors down; near the remaining four, we opened stands with bread from our cooperative bakery.

A few weeks went by and we felt that they were as good as beaten. Weinfield didn't even have enough work for one employee anymore, and the same held for the others. In the period of this strike situation, Weinfield sent for me, via his son, to come and see him. I came by and asked him what he wanted. He answered, "What is the practical purpose in continuing to strike? Perhaps we could settle?" I told him, "If you want to settle, just give a year's guarantee that you will not break the agreement, and pay us the cost of opening the cooperative bakery." "You'll never succeed in getting that out of me," was Weinfield's answer.

A few days later, I received a new invitation; once again Weinfield was calling for me. But this time, not to see him at home, but in a *rathskeller* (German salon) at Brown and Juniper Streets. I came in and encountered Weinfield with another man. I noticed that the other man was seated at a small table, such that he could see and hear everything that was going to take place. I acted as if I hadn't noticed anything. Weinfield invited me to eat; I declined. "Something to drink?" A glass of beer. "Smoke?" A cigar. Weinfield began speaking to me. "How long do you think, Weinberg, that you can keep your job as union organizer for the bakers? You're getting old and tired, and for whom are you laying down your life? For bums and drunkards? And what are you accomplishing with your strikes? You ruined me and you ruined the others. So wouldn't it be a good plan to end all this? Close the cooperative bakery and end the strike. You could do it if you only wanted to, and we would pay you well. I have here with me $500, and you can collect it on the spot, as soon as you agree to it."

I immediately suspected that this was a cunning attempt to discredit me before the workers, because the money was probably marked and the man would have been the witness. I answered him, "Here me out, Mr. Weinfield: if you were to collect all of the diamonds and gold hanging on your wife, and together with what you are carrying on you, and you were to add to that the buildings that you own, you wouldn't succeed in buying me, the pauper, off. You should be ashamed of yourself, to come in here and make me such a disgraceful proposal; and to top it all off, to malign the workers who made you rich through their toil. Whether it be five thousand or five million, you will never in your life be able to buy me off. I will continue to lead the struggle against you and the others. The weaker one will surrender. The struggle, you may be assured, will end only when we have a victory in all of the shops where we are now striking."

The result was that we, indeed, soon celebrated our victory in all of the striking shops.

Right after the strike, a certain Meyer Brooks became very active. His activism consisted of wanting to be an organizer for the bakers union. Seeing that he could not accomplish this so easily, an idea occurred to him. At that time the IWW was very popular with the numerous strikes it carried out in the textile industry, so Meyer Brooks started to make an attempt to organize a Jewish bakers union in the IWW, a rival to our bakers union which had belonged, since its founding, to the American Federation of Labor.

Under the guise of a revolutionary union name, he tried to coerce his way into becoming a union officer. To my great surprise and disappointment, the members of the bakers union were frightened by his attempt, and instead of opposing him, the union promptly hired him as an organizer. And since his ideology was never that of the principles of the IWW,[149] of which he was ignorant in reality, he immediately seized upon the offer and became a union organizer.

It hurt me bitterly. For so many years, I toiled and drudged to build up a bakers union, and a careerist comes along and barges into the union with force and treachery, and as a leader to boot. I immediately resigned in protest.

As a result of Meyer Brooks' installation as an officer in the bakers union, within a very short time, the bosses began doing whatever they pleased and the open bakery shops began to appear again. Fortunately, Meyer Brooks' reign over the bakers didn't last long, because he quickly reached his goal—he became and remains today a bakery owner.

One time, a man by the name of Koslovsky came up to me and invited me to give a lecture for a socialist organization. I walked into the hall, and two detectives showed up and asked Koslovsky who the speaker was. He pointed to me. They approached, one of them a Jew and one a Christian, and wanted to know what the topic of my speech would be. I told them that my topic would be "The Exodus from Egypt." The Christian detective looked over to the Jewish one and the Jewish detective explained to him, "That means the emigration of the Jews from Egypt." They laughed at the topic.[150] One of them asked me, "Where do you live?" I answered, "On a little piece of farmland." And they started laughing again. Then the Christian detective said to the Jewish one that he alone should stay and listen to me because he (the non-Jew) didn't understand Yiddish anyway.

After the lecture, the audience applauded and I noticed that the Jewish detective was also clapping. As people were starting to leave, he came up to me and said, "Weinberg, I know you pretty well, and I really enjoyed your speech; it was excellent."

And to this day, I still don't know why I was invited to give the lecture, and for what purpose, exactly, the two detectives appeared at the hall, and how it came about that a detective should applaud and praise my anti-religious speech.

That reminds me of a very funny occurrence which happened during the war. The Philadelphia waistmakers held a meeting in the Arch Street Theatre. The police director[151] sent police with an order not to allow anyone into the theater with any packages. I didn't know about that. On my way in, a policeman held up the bag I had with me and opened it up—in the bag were two mousetraps.

Surrounding Boston there are many towns with a large Jewish laboring population. When I was in Boston on a tour anyway, I went to visit several of these towns. On the train, I noticed a young man, whom I thought I had seen at my lecture in Boston. I arrived in Brockton, and he was there at the meeting. I left Brockton and traveled to Lynn, and he was also on the train. I got curious and asked him, "Why are you following me?" He answered, "I'll tell you the truth: I want to be a speaker. I have already given a talk. I am sure that I have the necessary ability to be a speaker."

I answered him, "There are two kinds of speakers: orators and lecturers.

"The orator, who gets up to give a "speech," has to know the subject about which he wants to speak; his voice must change often: at times loud and then becoming softer; not monotone, but full of enthusiasm, with feeling.

"A lecturer, however, is something else entirely. He must be prepared with facts and analysis about the topic he will deal with; he, as well as the orator, must have clear diction, and not speak in a monotone. They must speak assertively, not too quietly, and not repeat themselves. It also demands a good memory, in order to know how to cover the whole topic and when to end. For example, if you have to speak about the Paris Commune, you have to be familiar with all of the personalities who played a role in it, as well as the goals of the struggle. If you have all of these capabilities, then you will excel.

Having heard me out, he responded, "At the moment, I don't have all of those capabilities."

"If that is the case," I said, "then you would do better to become a life insurance agent."

Later I found out that he had followed my advice.

Chapter 13

Several years had passed since Isidore Prenner had left our movement, when we found out that he had opened an office—a fully-qualified engineer and lawyer.[152]

At that time, the well-known Austrian Zionist Birnbaum came to America.[153] When his evening in Philadelphia was announced, I saw that our former comrade Isidore Prenner would also be speaking at his lecture.[154]

I came to the gathering to see if it was really our Prenner, who had been one of the most active speakers and workers that our movement had had in Philadelphia. The moderator opened the evening with the following explanation: "In addition to the principal guest, we have another guest this evening, and he is so much more than a guest; a lost child of our great Jewish people has returned to his people. For many years he was lost on a path where he made fun of our prophets and God. But now he has left the activism which he conducted in the Philadelphia anarchist camp; he has come to us now and he is here with us now. I have the honor to introduce Engineer Prenner!"

And indeed our former comrade Prenner stood up and said: "That which the chairman has just told you about me is not in the least exaggerated; it is the plain truth.

"I came to America as a child of eighteen. I didn't know the Yiddish language; my entire learning consisted of knowing Russian. I didn't know a thing about our great prophets. I accidentally joined the anarchist party. I threw myself into the movement with my entire passion, into all its activities and struggles.

"Now my eyes have been opened. I had made fun of our prophets, not knowing who they were, but while teaching Jewish children, I discovered the greatness of our people's past prophets. Today's writers don't have anything new to say; they just repeat badly what the ancient prophets said. It became clear to me that only the Jewish teachings are the true lightbearer and guide in life, and from now on, I go together with my people, and if necessary, I will go to Palestine with my people."

A few years later I happened to meet Engineer Prenner, not in Palestine with our people, but in a coffee house in Philadelphia. I called out to him, "What's the matter, Prenner, don't you remember me any more?"

"What's up, Weinberg, are you still dedicated to the anarchist movement?"

I answered, "Yes, and you know, Prenner, I heard you speak at the meeting which Dr. N. Birnbaum held in Philadelphia." We sat down at a table and I conveyed to him the gist of his speech.

"Weinberg!" he cried out, "You actually remember nearly every word that I said."

I told him, "How could you go out there and claim that none of us knew anything? What about Gretch, Feigenbaum, Netter, Katz and myself? Didn't all of us learn Hebrew and indeed know about the Jewish prophets?"

What could he answer? He added that if I hadn't recounted his speech, he wouldn't have known how much nonsense he had spoken at that gathering.

Another of the activists attracted to the Jewish anarchist movement in Philadelphia was Max Staller. He, too, like our Prenner, had devoted his youth to our ideology. As soon as Max Staller had finished medical school and began seeing patients, he gradually began to pull back from his activity in the movement. Moreover, rumors began to spread that he campaigned among his patients about the necessity of circumcision.

It happened one time that we were sitting in a restaurant and Dr. Max Staller began in my presence to propagandize his new 'ideology'—circumcision. First he claimed that the surgery is necessary, because it is hygienic. A proof of that is that a lot of Christians allow the same operation. A second proof: the Jewish people are indeed the cleanest because they have a lower incidence of venereal diseases than any other people. I listened, but what should I answer him concerning his claim that much of his talk could be corroborated by many doctors and professors.

Just then, to my good fortune, who should pass by our table but Dr. Gartman, who was then an assistant professor of venereal diseases at Philadelphia's Jefferson College. I stood up and ran after him, asking him to come and give his opinion on Dr. Staller's claim. At first he refused; he would rather, he said, sit and read a book at home than sit in a coffee house. Finally, he consented. I introduced him to the others and explained the matter under discussion.[155]

Having heard me out, he thought for a while and then slowly began to give us his opinion. He explained, "If you have time I will bring a book with the authorities and facts from the last fifty years, and the proofs are exactly the opposite of those on which Dr. Staller is basing his claim. First of all, statistics show that tens of thousands of Jewish children have died each year as a direct result of the surgery due to the blood loss and the suffering caused by the operation. Secondly, what about all the Jewish children who survive the operation? It turns out that they are the weakest in comparison with children from all other races.

"The professors and authorities, on whom Dr. Staller supports himself, don't exist."

Dr. Staller remained seated, dejected and ashamed. However, he did certainly register one great victory: his surgery propaganda had an effect on one of our comrades—Y. Weinberg from Atlantic City. This naive father brought two boys aged eight and ten and allowed the bloody and brutal snipping operation to be performed.

A remarkable thing, or perhaps not so remarkable: as soon as one from our ranks had finished his studies and become a lawyer, doctor, or engineer, sooner or later we lost him. At least that is how it was in Philadelphia. New York had a bit more luck in this regard. The present-day Dr. Barbour was once a pants maker. While he was studying to become a doctor, he was still active in the anarchist movement; and during the time of the cooperative movement, he was for a time the president of the Cooperative. But just as with Dr. Staller, as soon as he went into practice, he distanced himself from us.

Later, he, like Prenner, went over to the Zionists, and, it turned out, from the Zionist path to becoming a Republican was not a great distance. The final stage for Dr. Barbour was, as all careerists end up, if not in the Democratic, then in the Republican Party, where he has found his peace to the present day.

Chapter 14

After having described the unpleasant characters in our anarchist movement, I can certainly devote some room to those of whom we can really be proud. Comrade Goldberg was such a person to the final day of his life.

Goldberg's only fault was to carry things to excess. That doesn't mean that he had even the smallest doubt about his claims. He himself was convinced that the social revolution would be coming, and it could come at any time. Here is one such incident that happened with Comrade Goldberg: The Russian Tsar drove the Jews out of Moscow.[156] One of the displaced Jews came to Philadelphia with a family of ten. Comrade Goldberg had a newspaper stand at that time. The fellow became acquainted with Goldberg and came to him for advice, asking what he should do with the few hundred dollars he had; in what trade should he employ it?

And our Comrade Goldberg answered the fellow, "Why are you wasting your time with your few hundred dollars? Don't you see that every little speck of a store is crushed by big capital? In France, they just beheaded the president." At that time (1894), French President Sadi Carnot was assassinated.[157] "It is only a question of three months, maximum, and we will all be equal in any case. Come with me to our meeting Sunday, and you will see."

The fellow heeded the advice of Comrade Goldberg and Sunday he came to our meeting. It seemed that Comrade Goldberg had truly not deceived him. First, he found about a hundred people in the hall; secondly, Edelstadt's songs were sung, actual revolutionary songs, and almost all of the speakers were speaking about the coming revolution.[158] What additional proof does the fellow need that the social revolution is awaited, and people are preparing themselves for it to come at any moment?

Following that first visit to our meeting, the fellow was convinced that Comrade Goldberg was right. Why should he bother going into business with his few hundred dollars, when

the revolution is coming soon to America. So he decided to wait
for the revolution. Six months later, Comrade Goldberg asked
the fellow, "What have you been doing?" The fellow answered
him, "What do you mean, 'What have I been doing?' You
yourself told me that the revolution was on its way and in the
meantime, I have eaten up the few dollars, and your revolution
is not here yet!"

I am sure that even when the fellow had told him about
using up the few dollars, Comrade Goldberg did not lose heart
and probably reassured him about the arrival of the promised
revolution, because he sincerely believed in it.

To say that Comrade Goldberg was a pauper would be an
understatement. First of all, he earned little, though he always
worked. Secondly, he had a wife and two children. Thirdly, his
wife was not the friendly sort, who would have understood and
appreciated Comrade Goldberg or any sort of radical
organization whatsoever. She behaved terribly toward him, as
one can imagine.

Religious fanaticism also played a great part in her
dealings against Goldberg, or better said, the religious
businesspeople in Philadelphia. They wanted to take revenge
on Comrade Goldberg, who was a very active atheist and the
main leader of the Yom Kippur balls. And they also hated him
not least of all for his famous saying which was popular among
the Jewish workers in Philadelphia: whenever a tragedy
occurred, "Thank God." The God-fanatics urged Comrade
Goldberg's wife to go to the Hebrew Charities for help. To the
question, 'Who is your husband?' she was told to answer that
he is an anarchist and doesn't want to work, and in the event
that he does happen to earn anything, he gives it all away to
the movement.

The funniest part of the tragic event was that with the help
of the Hebrew Charities, Comrade Goldberg was arrested—at
work—for not wanting to work in a shop. Of course, the judge
couldn't conceive of that and through the interpreter from the
Hebrew Charities, it came out that he did earn, but that he
neglected his wife and children and gave away his earnings to
the anarchists. When the judge started to question Goldberg,

he found out that he worked at Exter Brothers for six dollars a week and worked throughout the whole year. The judge, noticing that Comrade Goldberg could barely stand up, soundly cursed out his wife and remarked to her that it wouldn't hurt if she would help her husband make a living.

Some time passed after that and Goldberg's wife dragged him into court again on the same charge. To Comrade Goldberg's luck, it was the same judge as at the previous arrest, and she also came with the same troop from the Hebrew Charities and their interpreter. The judge stopped everything immediately and blasted Goldberg's wife with the warning that she shouldn't show her face before him again or he would arrest her; she had better help her husband.

Comrade Goldberg's mother was dying and she called for him. "I have four hundred dollars, saved penny by penny my entire life. You are my only child; give me your word that you'll say *Kaddish*[159] for me and the four hundred is yours."

Comrade Goldberg answered her, "Oh, Mama, you'll live on; you believe in God, after all. I am indeed a very poor man, but you can't buy *Kaddish* from me; not for four hundred dollars, nor even for four million. I also cannot promise you and then deceive you; my beliefs and convictions are not for sale."

Comrade Goldberg's mother died and at the cemetery the clergy came up to him and said, "Now, before laying her in her grave, at least say *Kaddish* once and we will give you the four hundred dollars your mother left."

And Comrade Goldberg didn't lack for an answer, as you can easily imagine.

Several years later, Goldberg found himself in New York. While I was sitting in Sholem's Coffeehouse in New York,[160] a man came up to me and told me that Comrade Goldberg was in dire straits, and furthermore he was terribly ill. I ran around immediately and collected about thirty dollars. I went to the address given, and found an old Jew. From my brief conversation with him, I realized at once that he was religious. I wondered aloud why Comrade Goldberg was living in the house of such a person. And the fellow responded directly, "If only all rabbis were as honest as Goldberg!" Unfortunately, I didn't find Goldberg at home; feeling a little better, he couldn't stay cooped up any longer and had gone out to the street. I couldn't wait for him, so I left. I sent him the thirty dollars from Philadelphia.

I didn't have any further encounters with our sincere Comrade Goldberg.

Comrade Lerman was a very lively and well-read young man. For the modern world, however, he was, as with all such types, an undesirable.

I ran into him once, and I took a good look and saw him so dressed-up you wouldn't recognize him. To the question, "What happened to you?" he let me in on a big secret: He was working at a newsstand and the newspaper buyers knew, of course, that he was an unbeliever and an atheist. Since Yom Kippur was approaching, one of the customers, a religious Jew, said to Comrade Lerman, "Do you go to synagogue on Yom Kippur?"

Comrade Lerman answered, "No." The fellow continued, "Nevertheless, you won't sell your share in paradise?" And he assured him that exactly the opposite was true; just let a customer appear. The fellow was horrified and trembled with rage. "If so," said he, "I am going to give you two ten-dollar gold pieces and you will sell me your share of the world to come." And Comrade Lerman wasn't at all disconcerted; he took the two gold pieces and sold his world to come, and for the first time in his life he dressed himself as a real dandy.

Speaking of selling paradise, I am reminded that I wasn't as lucky as Lerman. One time, as an organizer for the bakers union, I went in to see a bakery owner on the eve of Yom Kippur, and the owner asked me jokingly if I would sell him my share in the world to come.

"With the greatest pleasure," I answered him. We agreed on twenty-five dollars. He requested that I go with him to a lawyer and sign over to him my share in the world to come. I went to the lawyer at the appointed time; the bakery owner also came. He explained, however, that he had changed his mind on account of his wife. She had heard what he was about to do and had shouted at him, "Crazy, that you are; does someone like Weinberg actually have a share in the world to come? Of course he can be friendly and sell it to you."

I was not fated to earn an easy twenty-five dollars.

Chapter 15

Robert Wilson

Comrade Robert Wilson was another of the few truly intelligent people who was attracted to our movement. When the first big cooperative experiment was carried out, I was very eager to interest Comrade Wilson in the project, and when I explained it to him, he thought it over and then answered me: "I will tell you this, Weinberg: the cooperative idea is too idealistic to be a business, and too businesslike for an ideal. If it were a success, the jobholders would see to it that every idealist would be marginalized, if not entirely eliminated."

I answered him, "My dear Wilson, if we were to accept what you say as a criterion, what would happen if the anarchist ideology were to become a reality? Your argument could be used against doing anything. Why belong to a union if graft always turns up in the unions? Is it better, then, not to have a union at all, than a union with its inevitable graft?" And we continued arguing along those lines for quite a while. My reasoning didn't help, however. Comrade Wilson did not join the cooperative project. He didn't oppose the movement, however, as did several other comrades.

In 1906, in New York, I once walked out with Comrade Wilson after a meeting. The next day, the front page of the *Forverts* published the news that Comrade Robert Wilson had taken his life with gas. It was so unbelievable—here you are one day talking with a person and he doesn't give you the least reason to suspect that he will commit suicide. He goes directly home, turns on the gas, and puts an end to his young life. The news of Comrade Wilson's death greatly shocked all of those who had known him. Dr. Zhitlovsky, the whole intelligentsia which New York possessed at the time, came to the funeral. With Comrade Wilson's death, the anarchist movement lost one of its finest and most devoted members.

Harry Gordon[161]

After Czolgosz assassinated U. S. President McKinley, the
persecution of the anarchists was terrible. Wherever someone
was found to be an anarchist, the law enforcement officers ran
right over and threw the suspect in jail. And if the law
enforcement neglected to do that, "patriotic citizens" turned up.
We didn't yet know, then, about the Klu-Klan—"patriotic"
citizens dressed in white and wearing masks.[162] Comrade
Harry Gordon, who now lives in Mohegan Colony,[163] was at
that time in Pittsburgh, and many knew him as an anarchist.

Just then, when his girlfriend was in labor, Comrade
Gordon found out that a multitude of "patriots" was coming to
attack him. He hid himself, and the patriots, a couple of
hundred in number, arrived and discovered that they couldn't
find him. A few threatened to set fire to the house. Gordon
decided to save his girlfriend, and came out of his hiding place.
He told them curtly: here I am; do what you will with me.
Suddenly, one of the mob shouted out, "Let him go! He's
wearing a union badge, after all, and he's one of our brothers."

Comrade Gordon was actually a machinist, a member of his
union. Thus, the union badge truly saved him from a
premature death. It wasn't any better for us here in
Philadelphia. Our group had called a meeting to protest the
harassment. That was two weeks after the assassination. The
meeting took place in Washington Hall. As soon as I had
finished speaking, a whole squadron of police came in. The first
thing they did was to ask several people who the speakers
were. One of the law enforcers approached me as well and
asked: who was the last speaker? I answered him that I didn't
know, and he let me go.

Comrade Harry Gordon's life was saved by a union badge; I
avoided arrest by lying. Comrade Johann Most was persecuted,
as I already described, spending a year in prison, and dozens of
our comrades all over America were thrown in jail. This was
our penance for McKinley's assassination.

L. Moiseev (Leontieff)[164]

It was the fifth anniversary of the Philadelphia cloak makers union. A committee came to me, requesting that I bring a speaker from New York. Whom should I bring? Almost all of the well-known speakers had already come. It occurred to me to bring a new speaker, who had not yet been heard in Philadelphia: Moiseev. The celebration was supposed to be on a Saturday, so he might as well stay over till Sunday, and we, the anarchists, would have a New York speaker without "expenses." Comrade Moiseev came to Philadelphia and wanted to know what kind of a celebration this was and what he should speak about. I explained it to him and he became upset. Why did I choose him; what does he know about the cloak makers! What can he say about their anniversary? I told him, "Bandit, what do you mean you don't know what to say to them? Say a few words; we are getting $10 for your expenses, after all." Well, what choice did he have? We went to the hall.

The chairman started to introduce Comrade Moiseev and concluded thus: "The speaker from New York, himself a Russian revolutionary, will speak to you about the five-year struggle which our union underwent." Comrade Moiseev went up with his arms folded and was still thinking about what to say about the cloak makers' jubilee. Finally, he began: "Since you workers have a holiday today, and since you are all occupied with the needle trade, it would be appropriate to speak about how needles come to you. A mere fifty miles from Philadelphia, people set out for the underground depths. First, the earth is blown up with dynamite (an explosive material), and coal is brought out from the depths; the coal is loaded into rail cars; the coal is unloaded from the rail cars and used to fill boilers, and these same boilers drive the machines."

Suddenly, a man stood up and shouted out, "What's all this nonsense about mines and boilers and machines: what are you talking about? We came to hear about our five years, our strikes; that is what we want to hear about." Comrade Moiseev stood there confused and embarrassed, not knowing what to do: to continue speaking or not? Comrade Zahn ran up to me and asked me to go up immediately and say something about the jubilee. The chairman called me up to speak. Seeing the sort of impression his speech had made, Comrade Moiseev got down off the platform and didn't want to go on speaking.

Not having any other choice, I went up to say a few words. I spoke about the fact that the union had abolished the carrying of machines from shop to shop, as was once practiced in all of the needle trades. I told them how the union got the chicken pox and the measles, and so on.[165] The same man stood up and shouted out, "That is just what we wanted to hear."

After the celebration, on the way home, Comrade Moiseev really gave me a good scolding. And really, why did I have to drag him to such a jubilee, where he would be received like that? The next day, Moiseev gave a lecture, organized by our comrades, on the topic, "Professor Mendeleev's Theory." It was a wonderful analysis of Mendeleev's theory that the principle of free will works not only in chemistry, but in all other fields of knowledge as well. The listeners were really enthusiastic.[166] Our group promptly arranged a series of three lectures with Comrade Moiseev on the life and teachings of Mikhail Bakunin. These lectures were also a success. I was overjoyed, of course, especially when Comrade Moiseev's success followed on the heels of his big flop at the cloak makers' jubilee. Life is full of remarkable transformations! I recall the impression Comrade Moiseev made on those present at the first lecture. Dressed in faded, torn clothes, the audience regarded him as they had regarded me at my first appearance in Comrade Gordon's house in Pittsburgh. But right after the first lecture, the audience forgot about his clothes and found him inspiring. Several years later, Comrade Moiseev became well-known as a chief bridge building engineer in New York and along with his fame came wealth, and along with the wealth—a cooling off in his active participation in our movement. As far as I know, he still retains today the same ideological outlook he had in his youth.

Moyshe Katz

Few comrades in our movement today have any idea of the important role which Moyshe Katz played in our anarchist movement in America. (He has been living in Philadelphia the last 15 years and is editor of the daily newspaper *Yidishe Velt*).[167] The actual first *Fraye Arbeter Shtime*, which was founded in 1890, was chiefly edited and written by David Edelstadt and Katz. Earlier, Roman Lewis was the editor. Comrade Moyshe Katz kept up his activity in our movement for decades, writing and speaking. Katz had always been and remains one of the most delightful and sincerest speakers to be found among Jews. It is a real pleasure to hear him speak about literature or about any other topic. He is also an outstanding writer.

In 1905, when there was an outbreak of pogroms against the Jews in Russia, Moyshe Katz came out openly and declared himself a nationalist, which he remains to the present time. But to this very day, Katz considers himself to be the same anarchist as ever. Few people that I know in our movement demonstrate, in their relations with others, such a warm, loving, sincere friendliness, as everyone feels when they come in contact with Moyshe Katz. And it is also entirely possible that Katz would still be with the anarchists today if Saul Yanovsky had not become the leader of the movement.

At an encounter with Moyshe Katz (which happens quite frequently, because he has been in Philadelphia a long time), he said to me, "Weinberg, do you ever feel a pull to want to live in Palestine, see the Western Wall, the antiquities?"

I answered him, "Come with me to Fairmount Park, and I will show you a rock which is at least thousands of years old, and I'll also show you trees which must be hundreds of years old already, and who looks around at them?" Katz remarked, "You really don't have a poetic soul." I also managed to be present to hear Moyshe Katz speak at a memorial gathering for Comrade Hillel Solotoroff. They had been very good friends. Katz made a sincere speech, claiming that the Jewish anarchists didn't yet know what they had lost with the death of

Hillel Solotoroff. In Moyshe Katz' opinion, Comrade Solotoroff
was the Jewish Kropotkin. In my opinion, Comrade Solotoroff's
tragedy was that he couldn't go over to the nationalists
wholeheartedly, as Moyshe Katz had done. But at the same
time, he separated himself more and more from the anarchists,
because he felt that they disapproved of his nationalist
inclinations. He was never really accepted by the nationalists
as one of their own, and among us, the Jewish anarchists, he
was gradually less and less remembered.

Moyshe Katz has a son, Leo Katz; he is an electrical
engineer. During the World War, he was drafted into the
army. Just at that time, many unions called strikes in order to
get a greater share in the profits of the carnage. The
electricians' union was one of those which called strikes; Leo
Katz was sent to scab. He categorically refused to go, and was
promptly brought before a military court.

Before the court, he again refused to go and scab. One of the
people in the courtroom said, "Do you know that you can get
the death penalty for refusing to carry out our orders?" And
Leo Katz pulled out his union card and declared, "When I took
out this very same union card, I swore loyalty to my union
brothers, and I will not go and scab. You can do whatever you
will with me." After the war, Leo Katz received a dishonorable
discharge. But he is proud of his dishonorable discharge, and
his father, Moyshe Katz, even prouder.

Rudolf Rocker

For those who are at all familiar with the Jewish anarchist
movement, it is not necessary to explain in a separate
paragraph who Rudolf Rocker is. Born and raised in Germany,
Comrade Rocker was persuaded by the Jewish comrades in
London to help them revive the Jewish anarchist movement
there. With the almost constant assistance of Comrade
Frumkin, Rudolf Rocker, the German, became the first non-
Jewish editor of the London Yiddish weekly *Arbeter Fraynd.*
There is no doubt that thanks to Comrade Rudolf Rocker's

collaboration on the London *Arbeter Fraynd*, this weekly became the most famous anarchist organ, and remains so to this day. His articles and editorials breathed with fighting spirit.

In addition, the *Arbeter Fraynd*, with Comrade Rocker and the other comrades, began to press for the founding of the first Jewish unions in and around London. The impact of the *Arbeter Fraynd* was, one can rightfully say, worldwide. In Russia, people awaited unmarked envelopes containing the pages of the *Arbeter Fraynd*. In America, its arrival was anticipated each week. It was like that everywhere. In addition, Comrade Rocker and Comrade Frumkin brought the best writers from the world's literature to the pages of *Arbeter Fraynd* in translation. And another important thing: just as the *Arbeter Fraynd* was the first Yiddish newspaper to acquaint Jews with the greatest international writers, it also played the same role for a great many Yiddish writers, who made their debut in the London anarchist organ and later became well-known to the entire Jewish world.

So the decades passed, and finally, in 1926, my Yetta and I rejoiced that Comrade Rudolf Rocker was coming to America on a lecture tour. We would finally see him and have him with us. It is not necessary to describe Comrade Rocker's personality or his magnetic way of speaking. All who have heard him know and feel it. The greatest pleasure for me was when Comrade Rocker and Comrade Witkop came to stay with us at our small farm. We talked and reminisced about all sorts of past events in the anarchist movement, about the Russian Revolution, and so on.

When he found out how long I had been living with Yetta, he said to me, "You have been living for 27 years with one woman; a fine anarchist you are!"[168]

"Well, what about you yourself, with Millie?!" I answered. A long-awaited meeting with a dear, truly kind comrade and his lady friend, which left us both with lovely and pleasant memories.

Chapter 16

While I was lying in the hospital, someone once brought me a copy of *Mother Earth*, the English monthly anarchist journal published for many years by Emma Goldman. In that issue, there was an announcement by Comrade Isaak (the secretary of the longtime English-Language anarchist weekly paper *Free Society*) of plans to establish a land colony in California.

I became very enthusiastic about the idea and wrote a letter to Comrade Isaak, saying that I wanted to join as a member. Altogether, some 23 comrades responded; among them were Belgians, Germans and other nationalities, but the majority were Jews. We decided to send Comrade Isaak out to California to seek land. At that time, Isaak worked in Maisel's bookstore.[169] He quit his job and left for California.

It wasn't long before Comrade Isaak let us know that he had located a farm, seven miles from Lincoln and thirty miles from Sacramento. The farm had 160 acres of land; the fruits growing there were pears, apples, plums, peaches and grapes. Its price was $12,000. We agreed, and purchased the farm.

We worked out the plan for the colony ourselves. We would sell the produce collectively. Producing and dividing the income would be done according to the shares of each individual's contribution of products; that is, individualistically. We also dreamed of building houses for everyone and saving the best parcel of land to build a school with a large playground for the children.

When I was preparing to leave for the colony, I was still walking on crutches. The last day before leaving Philadelphia, I made a speech for the big trolley-car strike that was going on then.[170] I also made a speech in New York at Cooper Union, in the same physical condition. Then, Comrade Alexander Berkman took me to give a speech in Brownsville, and from there, I traveled to the colony.[171]

It didn't take long for me to sense that this idealistic endeavor, on which I and others had pinned so many hopes, was also doomed to fail. In the here and now of a new kind of experiment, it turned out that it was not so easy for city folk to arrive and become acclimated overnight to farming; farming demands much more physical labor than being a pharmacist or doing other, less strenuous jobs in the city.

If that big hurdle wasn't enough, another, more serious, obstacle came in the person of some four or five of the pioneering founders of the colony. They just happened to be the principal contributors in buying the farm. They soon became the main opponents of a cooperative farm, of working and living together.

One can imagine what was bound to become of such an idealistic experiment under the aforementioned circumstances: the same as happened with all of my romantic attempts at cooperative ventures in Philadelphia. After a two-year existence, the colony failed. The farm remained in the hands of the pioneers I just mentioned. Isaak still lives on the farm today.[172]

The only benefit that I received, thanks to the colony's existence, was that after six months of being there, I regained my full health.

Returning to Philadelphia from the colony, I took the opportunity and transformed it into a tour. I visited all of the more important cities; I even went to Calgary, Winnipeg, Montreal, Toronto—the principal cities in Canada. And I gave speeches in nearly all of the cities I visited. One thing became clear to me from the lecture tour: a speaker in the anarchist movement cannot make a living from giving lectures.[173]

When I began to scout around for work, I discovered that my youth was far behind me. I was getting old and was no longer able to work in a shop. What was there left for me to do, after I had devoted my entire life to the movement? Should I, in my old age, depend on charity and poorhouses—both institutions of the present order, which I had so bitterly and sharply opposed my whole life?!

I decided to buy myself a small piece of land and to do all in my power to support myself there by raising chickens. I found a couple of acres of land with a house on Welsh Road, near Willow Grove, Pennsylvania. To this day, the only thing that I

have to show from my cooperative ventures and dreams is—
this piece of land, called Weinberg's Farm, or, as some people
call it: Weinberg's Tiny Little Cooperative Colony.

As soon as I had settled on the farm, I immediately started
dreaming and scheming about new cooperative ventures. I
called a conference of the Jewish unions and Workmen's Circle
branches, and laid before them a plan to start a large-scale
cooperative movement.

At that time, an insignificant cooperative socialist grocery
existed at what was then the Labor Institute on Reed Street.
Well, B. Bikhovsky, who was then the manager of the
Philadelphia *Forverts* and main leader of the Jewish socialist
movement, came to the conference. What happened there was
that many unions and Workmen's Circle branches got together
and bitterly opposed the whole plan that I had brought before
them. Their main argument was: why should we start a new
cooperative movement, when one already exists? My logical
arguments, that the cooperative grocery was far from a
nonpartisan organization, but rather an explicitly socialist
enterprise, were to no avail.

The dead didn't allow us to make a living attempt. The
defunct cooperative grocery was victorious. Nothing came of the
conference. Their grocery didn't develop into anything; instead,
it failed completely.

At the same time that I bought the farm, I became better
acquainted with Comrade Yetta London, who has stood by me
and with me to this day, the most beautiful and dearest life
companion, with whom I truly share all of my joys and sorrows.
Without her loyalty, I would probably no longer be among the
living.

My only regret is that my age, and especially the long series
of failed ventures, frustrates me and curbs any desire I have to
make new cooperative experiments, here on the farm or
anywhere else.

Some time passed after I returned from the lecture tour in
1917, and again I felt a gnawing desire to do something in the
cooperative vein. So many times, my dreams had ended with

such a sad failure; still, who knew? It could be that this attempt would prove successful.

The new undertaking wasn't a cooperative house or a store, but rather, building cooperative houses for workers. I got the then-relatively-unknown rightists and leftists of Philadelphia interested in the work. Dr. Leow, an outspoken active leftist was chosen as the treasurer. The new cooperative venture aroused sympathetic interest among the workers. Many signed up as members. We quickly sold over sixty shares.

However, the battle between the new upstart socialists on the right and the left flared up again. The leftists lived only in the spirit of the recent revolution in Russia, and this also had an impact on our undertaking. Really, how could we compare our wanting to build cooperative houses for workers, on the one hand, with a social revolution of 150 million people, on the other hand? So it came to this: at a meeting of the new 'cooperative society,' someone shouted out, 'Weinberg the anarchist wants to lead us astray; he'll make us stop being laborers by transforming us into a *petite bourgeoisie*."

When I sensed that the workers' enthusiasm for the new plan was cooling off, I made another attempt to save the situation. I got Comrade Al. Brown, and went around with him to visit the carpenters union. We suggested to the union that they take over the whole plan of building cooperative houses.

There I struck up against a large stumbling block. Nearly half of the union members were themselves builders and contractors, and many of the remaining half hoped to become builders and contractors. Under such circumstances, could I have expected anything else but that they would employ every means possible to crush the cooperative plan? This time, it was not so easy to forget my disappointment. I decided not to make any more cooperative attempts. And to tell the truth, this was not easy for me to do. My life's companion, Yetta London, being many years younger than I and less disillusioned from cooperative attempts, strongly yearns for new cooperatives, and I am ruthless with all of her plans; I quash her desire to make any sort of cooperative venture.[174]

Chapter 17

In 1916 there was a convention of Jewish anarchists in Philadelphia at which they decided to send me out on an agitation tour throughout the land.

The agitation tour began on November 11, 1916, in New York. Comrade L. D. Abbott, the American anarchist, was also in the audience. When I asked him how he could bear sitting a whole evening, not understanding any Yiddish, he explained to me that it didn't bother him because he enjoyed seeing and hearing me speak.[175]

From New York, I went to Toronto, Canada. The lectures which the local anarchist group arranged for me were not a great success. They simply got very little publicity. I was more successful in Detroit, Michigan. The group advertised the lectures well, and the union meetings were also a great success.

From Detroit, I traveled to Chicago. I had great expectations from that city where we had made so many sacrifices. I expected at least to find a movement there in Chicago; what I found was a splintered, weakened movement and the progressive library—closed down. One single comrade, Sam Ogorsky, gathered together about twenty people to come to the lecture. Once again, the meetings arranged by the unions saved both my morale and my finances. After one of the union meetings, a young man got up and remarked, "This is the first time I have heard such a lucid speech at a union meeting." In Chicago, we visited the Waldheim Cemetery with the graves of our Chicago martyrs and of Comrade Voltairine de Cleyre.[176]

From Chicago, I traveled to St. Louis. There were actually a few comrades in that city who worked for the success of my meeting. Comrade Rothstein insisted that the hall, where I was supposed to speak, should be in an Italian rather than a Jewish neighborhood. Some fifty people came, however, even in an Italian neighborhood. And here, as well, I addressed a union meeting.

After St. Louis, I arrived in Cincinnati. Comrade Wolfson arranged the lecture for me there, at the opening of a library at the Radical Circle (Bund). They gave me three dollars. The cloak makers union arranged a meeting and two hundred people came.

Thus I once again had the wherewithal to travel onward, to Cleveland. There, of all places, an active group already existed. They also had a very good radical library. When they later gave up the library, they sent all of the books to the Philadelphia Radical Library, where they can be found to this day. The active leaders of the anarchist movement in Cleveland at that time were Comrade Rovner and his brothers. As soon as they found wives, they were lost to the movement. I arrived just at the moment when our entire movement was occupied with a birth control trial and court case, in which Dr. Ben Reitman (at that time Emma Goldman's manager) was also one of the accused.[177]

From Cleveland, I went to Pittsburgh. There I found English-speaking Jewish anarchists. The lecture was well-attended. Then I was taken to see their new club rooms. We found a room full of streetwalkers and young men. It gave me a shock. We sometimes saw high school girls in the anarchist movement, and now streetwalkers!

My lecture in Washington was a failure for both morale and finances. The same thing happened in Baltimore with the lecture organized by the group. The meeting organized by the unions, however, was a success, as everywhere. In Wilmington, the lecture was also successful.

In Philadelphia, the Radical Library completely forgot about me, as is typical in every family—the library didn't even arrange one lecture. However, the cloak makers didn't neglect me and arranged a large mass meeting in the Arch Street Theatre, which was very successful.

Then I traveled to speak in Lynn, Everett and Brockton. Since there were no cloak makers unions there, my lectures got the same brush-off as did most of the lectures arranged by our groups or by individual comrades.

I was supposed to end my tour in Boston. And just at that moment, the telegraph brought the happiest news in my life: the news about the outbreak of the social revolution in

Russia.[178] The Boston *Forverts* arranged a big gathering and invited me to come speak. Over two thousand people came. Speakers included the editor of the Russian journal *Novi Mir*, Meyer London, and myself. It is unnecessary to describe the excitement of the audience and the celebratory mood of the speakers themselves. Every one of us still remembers very well that great moment of joy and excitement that enveloped every soul where a spark of love for freedom glowed.

Since I am on the subject of the outbreak of the revolution in Russia, it is appropriate to recall the following: through my visit to Cleveland in 1916, I also met Comrade M. Volin and heard one of his lectures in Russian. In 1917, this consummate old Russian anarchist was among the first Russian revolutionaries to leave America and go back to Russia. He, together with a large group of our Russian comrades who had until then published the weekly newspaper *Golos Truda*, discontinued the newspaper, packed up part of the printing press, and left to take part in the first social revolution. Today, Comrade Volin is in Paris as an exiled political adversary of the Bolshevik state.[179]

Fedye, one of the best Russian comrades we had in Philadelphia, died battling for the revolution in Russia. We do not know the fates of many others. A few, like V. Shatoff, chose the "easier" way, forgot their anarchist outlooks, and became officials in the Bolshevik state.[180]

Chapter 18

When I was about to complete 30 years activism in the anarchist and the labor movement in 1917, the Radical Library in Philadelphia arranged two celebrations. The first was a public meeting at the American Theatre, where about 1,800 workers were present. Among the speakers were representatives from the cloakmakers union, the bakers union, and the vest makers union, as well as S. Schor, M. Cohen, S. Yanovsky and B. Vladek, and Comrade William Shulman[181] was the Chairman. Congratulatory telegrams arrived from all over the country and were read aloud. In the same evening a banquet was given where only 155 people were present. Over 500 wanted tickets, but the Colonial Cafe did not have sufficient room for everybody who wanted to come to the celebration.

At the banquet, more speeches were given and telegrams read. Here, however, was a little variation: Samuel Goldenberg,[182] who was in his youth a member of the London *Arbeter Fraynt* group, recited and played the piano. He also expressed his deep regret that I didn't dedicate my talent to the stage. Then the now-famous opera singer, the daughter of Comrade Braslau, Sophie Braslau, sang songs.[183] The restaurant was literally filled with flowers. At the conclusion, the bakers union presented me with a photograph of myself. I had, of course, spoken both times, at the meeting and at the banquet. I can't describe for you the mood that embraced me while hearing the speeches and telegrams about myself. I felt happy and satisfied that this honor was not given to Chaim Weinberg because there are so many Chaims in the world, but to Chaim Weinberg the anarchist for his activism in the anarchist and labor movement.

The youthful years gradually faded. New faces began to appear in our movement. And it truly made me glad. I received an invitation to come and speak in Yiddish at a May Day celebration, which the *Soyuz Ruskikh Rabotshikh* (which had at the time about 7000 members in almost all parts of America and Canada) had arranged together with the Italian comrades. The celebration was not at night, after work, but rather in the daytime. Comrade Shatoff spoke in Russian, a Comrade in Italian, and I in Yiddish, and finally, the chairman of the meeting in English.

The chairman was from the new young generation. Thus I was eager to hear him speak in English. He spoke very briefly, and said approximately the following: The history of the world shows that all revolutions begin with a minority. The rank and file follows after. If I were able to have 50 people who are willing to start the revolution, I would leave here immediately and begin working on it. I began looking at Comrade Shatoff, he at me, both our eyes looking for a policeman. Fortunately for all of us, there was not even one. I am sure that if the guardians of the law had heard the new speaker's naive, sincere speech, they would have cracked our heads and arrested us.

To finish the story of the May Day meeting, I will tell you a secret: The chairman, who gave the speech in English, was none other than he who now writes down this biography that I tell through him—Comrade Marcus Graham (S. Marcus).

Chapter 19

Social democracy, with its decades of activism and victories in the parliaments, turned out to be a complete failure. As for the working class, the workers are now more exploited, and in a more inhumane way than ever. The principal factor is that the "easier" reform path of social democracy squelched the workers' former spirit of protest and struggle.

Our "reform-orienters" in the anarchist movement could learn a lot from this.[184] They would save themselves a lot of effort and would transform anarchism into a new kind of social democracy. We can call protest meetings against violations of freedom, we can support reform movements indirectly, but pretending this is anarchistic activity is senseless.

Notwithstanding all of the disappointments that I have experienced and have described here, I am not a pessimist. I am certain that the anarchist ideology will become a reality in the very near future. This is not because anarchism has become a dogma for me, but rather this comes from my observations of human behavior. Studying everyone's psychology, I see that, both with animals and with people, there is an innate instinct for freedom. The anarchist theories were based on this same universal instinct: the yearning and the striving for freedom.

But the difference between unrestricted freedom and anarchist freedom is that I cannot be free until the whole society around me is free; i.e. when everyone has as much freedom as I have. On the other hand, we have studied the reasons for the fact that the greater portion of mankind lives in need and poverty. We ended up this way because one segment of society grabbed everything. From this same economic inequality, government and the state arose; economic inequality had to have a protector, so it created the state, and the state is therefore a direct result of this economic inequality.

Since we know from science that nothing is permanent— from the fact, for example, that slavery ended—therefore, the era of economic slavery must come to an end. All that we need to do is to be prepared with plans so that, on the day after the beginning of the social revolution, we will know what we are striving for, so that the same mistakes as were made earlier will not be repeated.

True, the current system of private property is a very old system, but there was never the large, organized working class which arose with the growth and spread of capitalistic rule in all areas of society. Therefore, I put all my hope on the workers: that they will be the factor which will bring us the new society, when the old one is destroyed. And although I know that, aside from the anarchist workers, there are other workers who are striving for the emancipation of mankind, I am still convinced that this will come only with the realization of our ideology.

We build up our whole philosophy on the voluntary uniting of workers. This is not a utopia, because we see that tens of millions of people are organized into unions, lodges and other associations—without prisons, soldiers, barracks, police, judges, and so forth. None of these associations have any compulsory laws, but rather only agreements. People come and join when they want to, participate as long as they want, and leave when they wish. The same thing can happen, in a greater measure, in all phases of social and political life, and this is my social ideal.

How do we come to the realization of anarchism? We must organize the worker as a producer through the unions, and as a consumer through cooperatives. We must bring communistic anarchism into the hearts and minds of the working class. Given that the capitalist society can never bring equality, it must maintain and expend millions on charities, prisons, and barracks; it must always have millions of jobless people, and the machinery drives the capitalist reign of inequality further and further.

Eventually we must arrive at a stage when millions and millions of workers are excluded from the possibility of nourishing themselves. This great army of the victims of capitalism will have to find a way out of the dilemma, and this will lead to an open revolution and to the building of a new society.

Events in world history have shown us that the capitalist class will never give up its position, and this will lead to a bloody struggle between the exploited and the exploiters, and it will begin the social revolution. I can hardly imagine that the capitalist class would agree to a compromise; to giving up a portion. Palliatives, such as political reforms, will not help to change the reality of the current inequality.

I know very well that it is very difficult to bring the anarchist-communist idea among the great masses, because anarchist doctrine is a spiritual doctrine, and capitalist rule simply destroys every little crumb of spirit people have; all it instills in people is materialistic ambition. That is why we have so few spiritual people.

Communism appeals to the body. Therefore I say to the comrades: when you go to the masses, emphasize communism first and foremost, and anarchism only later. This is because the great masses today possess nothing; because even those who already have a little house, furniture, a car —most of that is mortgaged or has money owed. Moreover, Karl Marx's saying is still relevant today: *The workers have nothing to lose but their chains.*

The anarchist-communist doctrine is an international doctrine. It is not just for one race or one nation, so our message must be brought wherever oppressed people are found. No Jewish, Christian, or any other national question exists for anarchist-communism; there is just one big question: the slavery of the worker. I believe that the worker question is the cardinal question, and there will be no end to all the troubles in the world until it is solved.

I am very optimistic. I don't think that the capitalist class can bring peace to the world. Despite all of the maneuvers in the capitalist society, with its League of Nations,[185] there will have to be wars in this world as long as imperialism, chauvinism, and exploitation exist. Every country seeks as much as possible to capture new markets, and this will bring about a situation where there aren't enough markets to exploit. Then must come the clash with all the other nations. The war of 1914 will be child's play when compared with the future world war.

It is the duty of all revolutionaries to unite and agitate against militarism in the coming world war. We must be ready, when it comes, to turn it into a worldwide revolution, which will be a preparation to commence building the anarchist-communist society.

That is one factor that will lead to a social revolution. Now here's a second. Today, in 1930, there are already over ten million unemployed in Europe, and the governments with the capitalists cannot find any means to decrease the growing army of jobless: it grows continuously. The day must come when the working class will demand a reckoning from the capitalist class, because the jobless will not be satisfied with charity.

We anarchists should bring the ideology of a future anarchist society to the masses. And these very masses, together under our influence, will initiate the worldwide social revolution and begin building the new society where freedom, equality, and brotherhood will become reality.

Appendix A

"Weinberg at Sunrise"
A passage from
In Quest of Heaven

By Joseph J. Cohen[186]

[Editor's note: Joseph J. Cohen (1878-1953), a Russian-born Jew, arrived in Philadelphia in 1903 and soon became active in the city's anarchist movement alongside Weinberg, the man who had won him over to the cause. His most lasting contributions there were to lead the re-establishment of the Radical Library as a full-on anarchist club in 1905 and the establishment of the Modern School on Sundays from 1910. Cohen and his family moved to New York in 1913, where he managed the Ferrer Center and then moved with it to Stelton, New Jersey in 1915. Cohen also founded Camp Germinal and managed it for two summers (1925-26) at Jamison, Pennsylvania, not far from Weinberg's little place in Willow Grove. From 1932-1940, this "Durham of the movement," as Voltairine de Cleyre had once called him,[187] led the Sunrise Cooperative farm community at Alicia, Michigan, some 95 miles from Detroit, in the Saginaw Valley. Cohen also served as editor for several anarchist journals over these years. There was no part of this great anarchist's career (here only briefly touched upon) that was not actively encouraged or shared in by Chaim Weinberg, until the scene related in the following passage. Although it took place about two years after Weinberg's memoirs were recorded (Summer 1933), it is only by this passage that we can guess why Weinberg omits to mention J. J. Cohen even once in his memoirs. It seems likely enough that there was mention of Cohen in the original form and then the falling out brought about a

*deletion before Weinberg's death, which was also long
before the memoirs appeared in print.]*

A very much different case was that of Chaim, who had
been my friend for many years and who, being over seventy at
the time he joined us, was our oldest member. Chaim, a cigar
maker by trade, was in his way, a very interesting kind of man.
He had received a scanty education, confined to the Yiddish
language, but he possessed a great gift of oratory which made
him known throughout the country as one of the best speakers
in our labor movement. He was crippled in one leg, he had a
bald, wedge-shaped head and a most unimpressive face, but he
would be transfigured the moment he saw an audience before
him. He had the knack of grasping a situation in which the
listeners were interested, and of presenting it to them in such
colorful language and such natural humor that he could keep
them spellbound for hours.

All his active life, Chaim had preached the virtues of
community organization and of a return to a natural life on the
land. He had made a number of unsuccessful experiments in
both directions, and had formed a number of communistic
households in Philadelphia and New York, all of which
foundered on the rocks of jealousy; one at least ended in
scandal, when a woman poured a pot of boiling fat on a
competitor who had alienated the affections of her husband or
lover.[188] He had also tried his hand several times at farming
and raising poultry, with very little success. And many years
before, he had lived in a colony which was organized in
northern California by Abe Isaak, the former editor of the
anarchist weekly *Free Society*. But this venture was not to his
liking, since it was based on individual holdings, and he
returned to Philadelphia, where he lived on an acre and a half
of low land on the outskirts of the city and once again
attempted, with disastrous results, to rear poultry.

Chaim was filled with enthusiasm by our project for a
collectivist community. To live out his last years in such an
environment—what could be better for a veteran preacher of
communism?

So he joined, paid his membership fee, and lent us $1,000 when we were short of money to complete our purchase. For our part, we were glad to have him with us, in spite of his age, for we felt certain that he would find some way of making himself useful, and we hoped that he would be of service in sustaining the spirits of the members when they became despondent. He might even, we thought, contribute to the smooth running of the community by acting as a kind of father-confessor, to listen to and discuss the real or imaginary grievances which, in time, would certainly arise among many so people.

Chaim arrived, looked around him to see what needed doing, and then took up the useful task of making cigarettes for the members of the community. His product was not as smooth as the machine-made article, but it was so much cheaper that even the most fastidious considered the saving worthwhile. But our hopes that Chaim would act as a stabilizing influence in the community were quickly doomed to disappointment.

It all arose over the first withdrawal from the community, which took place toward the end of the summer. The member concerned was a woman who had been one of the first and most devoted of our settlers. She had left her husband and two grown children in order to join the community, and for two months she worked hard in the fields and seemed very happy in her new surroundings. Then, a large bus load of visitors arrived from New York, and among them was her husband, who succeeded in persuading her to return to live with him.

That woman put her case to the board of directors, asking to have part of her membership fee transferred to a cousin who was a prospective member and was experiencing difficulty in raising the amount required. She also asked for a small sum to be given to her personally before she left. We had a definite understanding that no member, upon withdrawal, would have any claim upon the community, but, taking into consideration the circumstances of her case, the board decided to grant the woman's request and give her $100 in cash.

The decision had to be ratified by a meeting of the members, and there, to my surprise, the poor woman was roasted by the fires of Chaim's oratory—she was disrupting the community by causing the first break in the solid unity of our glorious and beautiful edifice, and so on, and so forth. I felt it my duty to try and counteract the impression his invective was making on the members, and to bring them to a more sober view of the case.

It was the first rift in our life-long friendship, and our first conflict in an attempt to influence an audience. I won the skirmish, but I lost the battle. From that time onwards, Chaim could never see any question from the same point of view as I. In the bitter struggle that took place during the following winter about the method of farm management, which I shall describe later in detail, Chaim joined the organized opposition, and when they were defeated, he left the community, saying that he was going on a short vacation and avoiding an announcement of his formal withdrawal.

His was the first withdrawal in a spirit of disruption, and it caused us a great deal of harm and unpleasantness. The weakness of human nature had, in our case, found expression in the strongest apostle of virtue, and the first real break in our pioneer ranks of communistic living was made by one who had spent fifty years of his life preaching the communistic gospel.

Appendix B

Chaim Weinberg

by Abraham Frumkin

Reprinted from *In the Spring of Jewish Socialism,*
(New York, 1940)

Among the bright moments that I lived through in London, belongs my becoming acquainted with the veteran of the American Jewish labor movement, Chaim Weinberg. That was a long, long time ago, in the first few years after my going over to anarchism, when both Weinberg and I were still, relatively speaking, very young. Both of us still dreamed the beautiful dream of a better world and looked to the near future with fresh hearts and with wide, open eyes. But he had "one over me," as they say in English—one possession which distinguished him over me, and over many others: he was blessed with humor, with an easy humor, which radiated from him and blended with his deep sincerity. A happy person, he made things easier both for himself and for others.

It was in mid-autumn of the year 1897. Our movement was half-asleep. Just a couple of years previously, the *Arbeter Fraynd* had ceased, and we lacked the necessary means to revive it. We had to make do with a scanty, insufficient oral propaganda. We went around depressed, unsatisfied, and the London fog bit our eyes and worked its way into our bones... Suddenly, Weinberg, the wonderful public speaker, landed upon us from America, and liveliness and good spirits returned to our hearts.

How did he come to London? Certainly, this was no pleasure trip. Weinberg didn't own any millions. He didn't even have his dacha yet, his palace, in Willow Grove. He was a worker: he sat in a factory, rolled cigars and made ten dollars a week. He devoted his free time to the movement, organized unions, participated in strikes, and addressed anarchist meetings. He had more than enough to do in Philadelphia, and it certainly wouldn't have occurred to him to make such a long journey.

But the London comrades requested that he come over for a lecture tour throughout England. This was, in those days and under those circumstances, an enormous undertaking, almost an adventure. Our entire circle consisted of nothing but poor people. Consider that when we had decided, at the end of 1895, to once again publish *Arbeter Fraynd*, we went to the table with twelve pounds (sixty dollars), and then we worked strenuously, giving every last penny to keep the paper going. There was free admission to the weekly meetings and lectures. In order to cover expenses, we used to take up a voluntary collection, which used to bring in a couple of shillings. So how could we, in such indigence, come to afford such a "luxury," the idea of bringing over a speaker from America?

Here is how it happened: As I recounted in one of the early chapters of my *Memoirs*,[189] the group *Arbeter Fraynd* had two personalities who couldn't live peacefully with one another, and frequently it used to come to clashes. These were Comrades Kaplan and Baron. Both serious, sincere people, but both were frightfully stubborn and oppositional characters. Kaplan was, in his time, the leading spirit, the tone-setter of the group. A popular speaker, who was seriously in love with the platform, he made himself very useful for the movement. But Baron was reputed to be an "idol-hater." In addition, he was a very impulsive person, with a hot temper, always unsatisfied, an eternal "fighter."[190]

It went along that way for a time. In the winter of 1897, after the *Arbeter Fraynd* had ceased, Baron managed to pick a fight with Kaplan. He gathered several of his close friends and founded a separate group, with the name "Likht un Lebn" (Light and Life). The then young comrade Aaron Mintz, who had a little earlier come to London and had become known under the name of A. Bonoff, promptly joined this new group.

I can't recall what actual work the group Likht un Lebn did in the early period of its existence. I only remember that its activity and initiative, its plans for oral and written propaganda—all this interested me and attracted me to its circle; and there, among other things, the plan to bring over a speaker from America originated.

Baron came up with the idea. He claimed it would bring a bit of life to the movement. It would attract new and greater masses of people, who seldom or never came to our meetings. But it was easy to talk, to make plans. Whom would we bring from America?

Just then, Voltairine de Cleyre happened to be visiting London.[191] She became interested in the work of the Jewish comrades and had visited our meetings a few times, in the Jewish quarter; and in midsummer, when the Jewish comrades arranged an excursion to the famous woods Epping Forest, Voltairine was with us. We spoke with her about our movement and among other things, told her about our plan to bring over a speaker from America. She made it clear to us that this was not such an easy thing to carry out. Nevertheless, she thought there was one Jewish speaker whom we would be able to bring over for a lecture tour. This was Comrade Weinberg, from Philadelphia. She also gave us an idea of what a wonderful speaker this Weinberg was.

The only one who was strongly opposed to this plan was Kaplan. He claimed that this was too great an undertaking for our means. Aside from that, it wouldn't bring any proper income to the movement. The effort and money that it would cost could be better spent on our written propaganda, on the revival of *Arbeter Fraynd.* But Baron had already made his decision, and under his influence, the Likht un Lebn group contacted Weinberg in Philadelphia.

Weinberg answered succinctly: "I am a cigar maker. I earn ten dollars a week. I must have this to feed my child, a boy, a year and a half old. If you can guarantee me this ten dollars a week, I am willing to come to England."

We didn't delay; we collected money for a ship's ticket, sent it to Weinberg with a guarantee that he would receive two pounds a week for the whole time that he would be in England. Then we waited impatiently for our guest.

We (Sarah and I) lived then in the West End, in the
western part of London. One forenoon, there was a knock on
our door. When I opened it, there appeared the slender image
of Aaron Mintz, with his blond head of hair and his smiling
face. Behind him stood a man with a cane in his hand. I didn't
have to wait to be introduced; I knew who it was. I immediately
realized that Mintz, the energetic activist and leader, had
brought to me the guest from America, Comrade Weinberg.

We spent an hour or two together. What did we speak
about? I can't remember exactly and I couldn't relay it exactly.
I only know that it didn't even take five minutes for Weinberg
to become so familiar, that it seemed to me that I had known
him for who knows how long. And he did most of the talking; he
talked about his experiences in the American Jewish labor
movement, recounted episodes and described all kinds of
characters. Thereby, as was his custom, he went from joking to
seriousness. As I observed him, sitting like that, with his cane
in his hand, and speaking with enthusiasm about the
movement, he seemed to me like our forefather Jacob, who
crossed the Jordan with his cane: thus, it seemed to me,
Weinberg was ready to stride into the social revolution. And if I
recall correctly, I wasn't any less ready than he.

But the social revolution was in no hurry; it was still
awaiting us. Meanwhile, one had to worry about all kinds of
petty things: earning rent money, buying coal, paying gas bills,
and—preparing the meetings for Weinberg.

We rented, for several occasions, Christ Church Hall, a
sizable hall on Hanbury Street, in the middle of London's
Jewish quarter. The first meeting was scheduled for a Friday
evening. Here I must recall with a painful feeling the
stubbornness of the group *Arbeter Fraynd,* with Kaplan at its
head. It went so far that they didn't cancel the weekly meetings
which took place regularly in Sugar Loaf, also on Hanbury
Street. A lecture by Kaplan was announced for that same
Friday evening that Weinberg made his first appearance. Of
course, Sugar Loaf was empty.

But Christ Church Hall, which held about five or six
hundred people, was packed. The audience awaited the guest,

the speaker from America. When Weinberg entered the hall, accompanied by a few friends, a whisper was heard, "There he goes." One could discern a kind of disappointment on many faces, especially among the women. His gait, his figure, and perhaps also his smooth, bald head - all of this, apparently, didn't impress them. But ten minutes later, when the meeting was opened and the guest got up from his chair and started to address the audience, all eyes were fixed on him, as if they suddenly saw another person entirely. I myself went closer to the platform, and—truly, it was a sort of transformation, another Weinberg. As if he had become taller, and more powerfully built, and—more handsome.

His topic that first evening was: "Greetings from America." I remember that. Everything after that is unclear, not recorded in my memory. And my memory is, after all, the one and only source which I can make use of in writing this chapter. I would have liked to convey something of the content of Weinberg's first lecture which held the several hundred listeners enthralled, and with his pictures and descriptions brought them from comedy to seriousness, from laughter to profound thought. But there is not one sentence, not one printed line to turn to for "reference" to refresh my memory. It was Weinberg's "luck" to come to London when the Jewish anarchists didn't have a newspaper, and not even the briefest report appeared about his tour and his great, successful meetings.

But I remember very well the impression his manner of speaking made on me and on so many others. I sat and thought: Here I am hearing for the first time someone who is not speaking from a book and repeating ideas gotten from newspapers, pamphlets and books. That doesn't mean that Weinberg didn't read. Of course, he was well versed in everything that was published then in Yiddish on socialism, anarchism, atheism, and other "isms." Yes, Weinberg was really a diligent reader, but he "re-cooked" the ideas: took the essence, the quintessence and told it in his way, with his easy, folksy style, with his original proverbs and with his own illustrations, with comic and tragic images which he drew from life, from experience, which he could so masterfully depict—a wonderful public speaker.

I don't know exactly how many times Weinberg spoke in London. Several weeks after his arrival, I decided to travel to America. I bought a ticket, but when I got to Liverpool where I intended to board the ship, I was detained, as I recounted earlier, by the local comrades, who were planning to publish an anarchist newspaper in Liverpool.

Meanwhile, Weinberg had concluded his lectures in London and came to Liverpool, where the anarchists had arranged two big meetings for him. A couple of interesting episodes remain in my memory from one of these Liverpool meetings.

The same day that Weinberg was supposed to give his first lecture, he met with a *landsman* of his, an old friend who owned a large bakery. They spent an hour together in a restaurant and spoke about the old country, recalling the past life in their town. A couple of hours later, Weinberg found out that a bitter strike was going on at the shop of his *landsman*, the bakery owner.

At the meeting that evening, the landsman was in the audience, in the hall. Weinberg, in his speech, touched upon the question of property and tried to show that animals don't have this instinct; they don't know from property.

When it was time for questions, Weinberg's *landsman* requested to have the floor and asked: if animals don't know from property, how is it that a dog lies at the door and attacks every stranger who tries to enter? Weinberg took up the question with a special satisfaction. He repeated it, and explained that it is not such a mystery. He has greater wonders to tell from America. There, for example, a parrot sits by the cash register in a beer saloon, and makes sure that the one serving the beers doesn't, heaven forbid, steal a few cents. And in case it doesn't register the correct total, the parrot lets out a scream, and the boss comes running. Yes, yes, such wonders are to be found in Columbus's land.

"But," Weinberg concluded, turning directly to the questioner, "the dog which lies at the door and doesn't let any strangers in, is not a dog, but rather a boss."

A thunderous laughter was heard, and all eyes turned to see the embarrassed bakery owner.

A while later, came a second question. In the gallery a young man stood up and said with a sonorous *gemore*-tune: "And how is it going with the struggle for existence?" That was all, and he sat down again in his seat. From the hall, people looked up with curious glances at the gallery, and several people recognized the young man. It was a Jewish student from Oxford University.

I remember how uncomfortable I felt. I had an idea about Weinberg's "learning," about his knowledge in such matters, and I thought: how is he going to deal with this student?

But, "God sends the cure before the disease."[192] A couple of years before that, two articles by our late friend Dr. Hillel Solotaroff appeared in the anarchist journal *Fraye Gezelshaft* (Free Society) about Kropotkin's work *Mutual Aid* which had been published in English. Weinberg now put to good use these same two articles that he had read and preserved in his memory. He took his time, explained in his simple way Darwinism, on the one hand, and Kropotkin's theory of mutual aid on the other. The student was so happy that he waited for the speaker after the lecture, shook his hand and thanked him for his excellent answer.

At the beginning of 1899, I once again met Weinberg—in America. Philadelphia was, at that time, a lively center of our movement. There, it was easy to bring together a large audience to come to an anarchist meeting. One only had to have some sort of a "new face," a fresh person with a new name, or an interesting topic. One day, our late Philadelphia comrades Robert Wilson and M. Perlman, cast an eye on me and decided to make me their "victim." They kept after me about coming with them to Philadelphia to give an anti-Zionist lecture.

Political Zionism was then a hot topic—a good topic—for a mass meeting. Wilson and Perlman knew that I am a Palestinian, born and raised there. Who else knew the situation there better than I? And who, besides me, could come out so well against Zionism?

I explained to my two dear friends that I would be happy to accept their invitation. However, I am not an orator; I have never addressed any meeting. I never even speak a word at the smallest gathering; I sit at the side and remain silent. Indeed? They had some advice for me: I should write out my lecture and read it aloud. That's quite a job!

I fought and struggled, like a lamb against two lions... until I gave in and started preparing the lecture.

It took me a couple of days to search out the material: statistical data about Palestine, its geographical situation, its territory, its suitability for colonization, its population, and so on. I wrote up a long lecture with the title: "Can Zionism Be Realized?" and one Sunday afternoon, I came to Philadelphia ready to deliver it.

The meeting was in a big hall. There I found an audience of several hundred people. The moderator was Comrade Weinberg. He gave a short speech and introduced me as a great expert, a specialist in Zionism—excuse me, I mean anti-Zionism. Then I read my lecture aloud. It took almost an hour and—why should I hide it here?—the content, packed with figures, was not very exciting. But I was lucky. They patiently heard me out.

When I was finished, my dear moderator wasn't remiss and invited the audience to pose questions. I leaned over to him and said quietly, "Rascal, what are you doing? I am no lecturer; I won't be able to answer." But he did his thing. Questions were asked, as usual, empty, foolish questions, but also very serious and important ones. I thought to myself: it is a shame that they will remain unanswered and Zionists will have something to mock.

As the well of questions began to dry up, I saw that the moderator was turning in his chair and looking at me, as if to say, *Well?...* Then he got up and explained that since I am not a lecturer, he would himself try to answer the questions that had been posed.

I hung my head, so the anxiety on my face wouldn't be visible. I pitied those who had posed questions, because how was the moderator supposed to get the answers that they could and should expect to receive? But my pity was unnecessary. Weinberg's joking "answers" satisfied both the large audience, and the questioners, and the hall resounded with applause.

Years went by, varied years: good years and bad, hopeful years and overwhelming years. But I don't remember a single moment when I encountered Weinberg in a troubled, doubtful mood. I don't know of another, in our radical circle, who tried as hard as he did to realize our ideals, to move from theory to practice. One attempt after the other: communes, cooperatives. And he experienced one failure after the other. But that never discouraged him. How long has it been since I saw him so enthused, when he came up to the office of the *Fraye Arbeter Shtime,* and bade us goodbye before leaving for his new ideal world, for the collectivist-cooperative experiment in Michigan?! I envied him. I envied this elderly man who could be as enthusiastic as a child when he saw the chance to create a better and brighter environment. I envied his courage, and the ease with which he could shrug off every failure, every disappointment, and continue to seek and continue to try.

A happy man, an optimist to the end of his long, shining life.

Appendix C

Weinberg: An Historical Figure

By Samuel Polinow[193]

Excerpts from the essay in *Man!* March 1939 (published in English)

Death has called upon one of the greatest figures that ever lived in the anarchist movement. The cruel end came to Chaim Weinberg, the most beloved and respected comrade, on January 26. He died in a hospital near Philadelphia at the age of 79.

The passage of Chaim Weinberg, though he died at the age when all life must return from whence it came, was nevertheless an unexpected shock to the radical circles of Philadelphia. For Weinberg was an historical figure in this community, where he devoted most of his life to organizing the workers in many trades in strong unions and to the preaching of his ideal philosophy: Anarchism[...]

The history of the Jewish labor movement in America, particularly in the city of Philadelphia, is closely connected with Chaim Weinberg. The Jewish trade unions of Philadelphia, which are now strongly organized and are in a position to command better living conditions for the workers, owe much to the effort of this "labor agitator" whom death has now taken from our ranks. He not only worked untiringly to help build these unions, but taught and reared the workers of the needle industry, the baker industry, the carpenters, and many of the various trades, to be and remain conscientious union members.

Fifty years of his life Weinberg gave to the cause of the working class. Their cause became his ideal aim in life. Their plight was his plight. Their struggle was his struggle. He marched with them in victory and he encouraged them in defeat. He was their spokesman, their father, their champion for a better world to live in.   Rather than to illustrate by scientific facts the functioning of an anarchist society as laid down by authors of anarchist philosophy, he employed a most unique and simple method to convince his listeners of its possibility. He spoke to them as man to man. To a group of bakers he would say: "Do you think a senator is as useful to society as any one of you bakers?" And to the needle workers: "Do you think a governor could make as good a pair of pants as you can?" And to others: "Do you need a policeman to tell you when to go to sleep?" [...]

Age gradually began to tell on this hard-bitten soldier of the masses. No longer could he "take arms against a sea of troubles." This is the destiny of all men. And so, nearing the age when Time calls all men from the scene of battle, Weinberg retired from active service and settled down on a small piece of open prairie surrounded by brushwood and farm trees. With the assistance provided him by some trade unions in gratitude for his past favors, he made his home there.

A new chapter has since been written in the life of Weinberg. His name attracted visitors from every part of the country. People from far and wide made pilgrimage to Weinberg's Yasnaya Polyana,[194] as some were wont to call it. A visit to Weinberg meant a spiritual gratification, for he never let a moment pass without intellectual discussion. Like the wise Athenian, he would be sitting on a reclining chair, and invariably would open a discussion that would either date back to ancient Greek sophistry or present-day economic depression. The logic and reasoning with which he treated every subject could only equal the mind of a genius.

It was an interesting period for the old sage. He derived unlimited pleasure in this secluded place where he could give himself up to intellectual meditation. From time to time he left his peaceful abode and went on a lecture tour. From time to time a union would call upon him to deliver an encouraging speech to striking workers. In 1933 he joined a cooperative colony that was organized in Michigan, but he always returned to his favorite chair on the farmland. There he found his friends and comrades, with whom he always talked of the great disappointments present-day Fascism has wreaked on thinking humanity, and at the same time instilling in them new hope, new encouragement in the fate of the coming social order.

In the last stages of his life, the old veteran felt the inevitable end approaching. He still greeted his visitors with the customary, wide "H-e-l-l-o!" He still made every effort to converse with them on the political affairs of the day. Spain, Barcelona, Fascism were now uppermost in his mind.[195] How he wanted to cheer up those who have lost faith in the great struggle against reaction! It was to no avail. The great spirit was declining. Life was ebbing away. Then on the night of January 26, the inevitable end came.

The comrades and friends will probably forget the flesh that lived in this human frame, but the memory of his spirit will remain with them forever.

Appendix D

Chaim Leib Weinberg

By Yud Lamed Malamut

Excerpt from the *Fraye Arbeter Shtime*[196]

When I scan through, in my mind, the history of the Jewish
Labor Movement in America, the image of Chaim L. Weinberg
stands out among the labor leaders and activists floating before
me. He is one of the greatest of those who contributed to the
development and enlightenment of the worker. He stands
before me a unique, one-of-a-kind, remarkable person, who
distinguished himself from all the other leaders. It is possible
that the others indeed spoke in a more polished language,
while Weinberg's language was plain and simple. But one could
doubt the genuineness of their words because their sincerity
was questionable, while Weinberg spoke from the heart, with
fire and soul, and his words were *devarim ha-yotsim min ha-
lev.*[197]

He used to pull us along with his words; he drew us in and
won our fullest confidence. He stood before us as a friend of the
workers, a folksy person who lived as "we the people," who got
bloodied for the worker, and who was himself a worker (a cigar
maker).

The writer of these lines was privileged to know Weinberg
since the beginning of the century when, after 1900, (almost
fifty years ago), we met in Philadelphia. He was already then a
recognized leader in the anarchist movement. After all, at that
time we thought that we were on the verge of the social
revolution. It "must and will come." He also played a leading
role in the trade union movement, which was then at a low
point. The bakery workers, especially, were then lying, as
Weinberg would have expressed it, "nine cubits in the ground."

If the bakery workers indeed attained better conditions, they have Weinberg to thank for it. But he was also a dreamer, a person with a multifaceted power of imagination, and at the same time, a realist. He knew that the enemy, the capitalist, could not be driven away with a single blow, with a trade union, because the capitalist strikes the workers with a thousand rods. The capitalist not only takes the 'cream' of the workingman's product through barter,[198] but he is also the worker's landlord, his clothing maker, his baker, and his shoemaker; the worker can therefore never satiate the "damned overfed capitalist."

That period, forty or fifty years ago, was really bursting with utopian ideas; and the idea of cooperatives became popular in Philadelphia even more so than in New York, thanks to Weinberg. He was really passionate about the cooperative ideal, the idea of having various cooperatives: hat stores, shoe stores, bakeries. He didn't doubt that they would be successful, "because the worker has to wear hats and shoes, after all, and must have these same articles for his wife and children." If so, then why not also have "cooperative bakeries, clothing stores for men and women, our own restaurants and finally, our own banking businesses as well?"

In addition, Weinberg possessed the magnetic power to stand up and speak and convince people with simple logic, with common sense, and thereby inspire people. Getting up and speaking about the Paris Commune, for example, he painted such fresh and lively images of the communards, that one felt oneself ready to go help start the revolution.

And another thing: Weinberg was a person with an inexhaustible fount of good-natured humor: a hearty humor; not a stinging, bitter humor, but a sort of good-naturedness which made you smile and often start laughing out loud.

He wasn't a homebody in those years, but moved around like quicksilver. He believed in agitation and traveled around a lot, making a tour of America and Canada every year. Now, Jewish speakers come with a price; that is, they get paid. They stay in hotels, and travel to and from the train with a taxi; but not Weinberg!

Traveling around America, I met Weinberg in a number of American and Canadian cities, and I always marveled at how frugal or impoverished he was.

Even Emma Goldman was already staying in hotels, but I met Weinberg in Cleveland, for example, in a commune among Jewish fellows: Rovner, Witkowitz, Cohen, Glickman, Schwartz—all working drudges, and Weinberg was in seventh heaven among them.

Winter. Outside there was six feet of snow, the windows were covered with ice, you wouldn't want to get out of bed; but Weinberg, older than all of us, got up first, made a fire, and warmed the house before everyone got up.

"Weinberg, what are you doing?" I asked.

"I am a freeloader, after all," he answered me. "I don't have to speak until Friday, and I have already been staying with them for three days, eating and drinking, doing nothing, and they are working, they are feeding me. They will soon have to get up for work, so the least I can do is warm up the house a bit for them." I seldom saw such responsibility toward his fellow man from a Jewish speaker in those days. He actually got the house warm, put up the coffee, and served the comrades.

Weinberg had a lifelong dream of remaking the world. He believed that, just as a society is composed of individuals, so one cannot remake the world without starting with the individual. And if one is starting with the individual, one must indeed begin with oneself.

He reformed his own life over the years. He believed, no he was convinced, about the idea of colonization, which always attracted him to farms. Wherever any attempt was made, any experiment in colonization, he was always one of the "first ten" to join in, to collaborate, to live in the colony. It was thus in Stelton, New Jersey, in Sunrise, Michigan, and elsewhere.[199] Possessing a healthy sense of humor, he was always the first to recognize the pettiness and hollowness of those persons who quickly started "managing" and used the cooperative idea for their own ambitions.

But instead of fighting with the whole community like Korach, as others began to do, throwing pitch and sulfur on the movement, Weinberg behaved more cleverly and more decently. He always claimed: just because Berl or Shmerl behaved uncivilly, does that mean that the idea is wrong? It means no more than that this or that person is not yet adult enough to live with an ideal which will be accepted in the future. But the idea is right!

Nobody could say that Weinberg neglected the interests of the workers. He lived a long, active, energetic life. New times have come: wars, turmoil, revolutions... Chaim Leib Weinberg aged physically, but did not become old in spirit. He was lived a full measure of years, experienced much, had many disappointments, didn't have much joy from the labor movement. But he remained young in spirit until the last day of his life.

Appendix E

Chaim Weinberg, The Anarchist Speaker

By Leon Kobrin[200]

This appreciation was first published in the *Morgn Freiheit*
(New York) in 1942.[201]

The members of the Knights of Liberty group were busy
every night with gatherings and meetings, and with
distributing literature wherever they could. And they couldn't
let the social democratic meetings go by without a proper
debate.

Our regular speakers were two Weinbergs. One Weinberg
looked like an intellectual. He was always neatly dressed, wore
a respectable coat, a fine suit, shiny shoes and a pince-nez, and
he always spoke a very Germanized Yiddish with a lot of
shouting. If I am not mistaken, he was a cutter of menswear by
trade. The other Weinberg appeared to be the very opposite of
an intellectual, very *We the People,* a stout fellow with broad
shoulders and dressed any which way, often very sloppily.
Aside from that, he just wasn't physically handsome. He had no
hair on his head, he limped on one leg, and he peered out from
half-blind eyes. However he did have a nice, high, and (I would
say) intelligent forehead. He was a cigar maker by trade.

Aside form those two, we had additional speakers such as
Gretch and Barbour, a young man with one eye (later, I believe,
he studied medicine). Also Sam Gordon, an intimate friend of
the famous Voltairine de Cleyre; he too studied medicine later
and had a practice in Newark, New Jersey. Of all these
anarchist speakers, even including the speakers who
sometimes came down from New York, the lame and half-blind
Chaim Weinberg made the deepest impression on me. He was a
thoroughly folksy sort, a *naturphilosoph* type, and what a
speaker! He didn't get overexcited when he stood before an
audience; he didn't try to win the audience over with

revolutionary foot-stamping and breast-beating, or by shouting out curses and imprecations on capitalistic heads at the top of his lungs, or by shouting 'hurrah for the social revolution.' Most speakers did, both the anarchists and the social democrats, among the intelligentsia.

He spoke calmly and coolly in a simple, vernacular speech, which came from his mouth so soft and supple, so colorful and with so much humor that Sholem Aleichem himself might have been jealous of him. I ran to hear him whenever he was speaking. I loved to hear his gentle voice and his flowing speech and the ideas he projected, some simple and some original, and the clever parables he told, which had the audiences rolling with laughter.

More than once, many years later while reading Maxim Gorky's *My Universities,* I recalled this same Weinberg and thought to myself how similar he was to the perceptive and marvelous image of a people's philosopher that Gorky describes there. It seems to me that I can still see him today with his shiny, wide, and intelligent forehead, in the local on Pine Street in Philadelphia: how he is standing there on the platform, a little inclined to one side on account of his lame leg, and I hear his voice and the particularly comical intonation with which he was describing the worker and the whole contemporary social order, and images come alive for the listeners in the local, images created by a real word-master, some tragic in their comedy and some comic in their tragedy, such that every so often his voice is drowned out by a storm of laughter. Indeed, he was a wonderful wordsmith, with a tranquil smile through which he regularly launched his original ideas.

This same Weinberg used to tell me in those days, "don't be so zealous; a fire which flares up like that must quickly burn itself out. I'm afraid that you will not be with us for much longer." For a time we were very close friends and he was especially interested in me. At that time, he once brought me to one of his friends who had a small cigar factory somewhere around Girard Avenue, (the comrade was a bit of an anarchist), and that fellow taught me how to clean tobacco leaves from their roots so that they could be used for the cigars. That is, I became a stringer in his tobacco factory and I earned three dollars a week. For me, that was a lot of money, particularly in those days when things were getting worse and worse, approaching the crisis of 1893. Anyway, it was sufficient for room and board with my landlady Gitl.

Every week I used to read Johann Most's *Freiheit* to Weinberg when it arrived from New York, and he always listened to my reading with his eyes closed. The paper arrived on Saturday, and I usually read it to him on Sunday afternoon. He lived with a woman, or at this woman's house (I don't remember precisely), in an old wooden house somewhere in a back alley, and for a time I used to used to go there every Sunday afternoon. He was always waiting for me at the entrance to the house, waiting for me like my missus Gitl used to wait for me when she had a letter to be addressed in Russian, to send to her son in Vitebsk. And when he saw me with his half-blind eyes, his clean-shaven face smiled good-naturedly and he hurried into the house in front of me, limping on one leg.

Then we both sat down in a private room inside the house. There, lying on the bed and on the floor around the bed, were Yiddish pamphlets and Yiddish newspapers that Weinberg had read earlier. Yiddish was the only language he was able to read. I don't know if he was even able to write in Yiddish. He was well able to understand the language of Most's *Freiheit*, when somebody read him that (German) newspaper.

"Come on, read!" He passed me the new issue of the *Freiheit* he'd gotten ready when we sat down at the table, and he leaned on the table with both elbows, and he closed his eyes and listened as I began to read. Curiously, once while he was sitting there listening with closed eyes, it seemed to me that he was looking at me through his intelligent forehead and was also listening to my reading with his forehead.

Incidentally, once I had the same impression from another unusual personality: actually from the poet Chaim Bialik,[202] when we spent an evening with him at Jonah Rosenfeld's home. He say there with his eyes closed the whole evening and he also spoke in parables and analogies, and all this sprang out from a very deep source which, it seemed to me, was hidden somewhere behind his forehead, over his closed eyes. I had the impression the entire evening that he was looking at all of us and also listening to what we were saying through that same forehead, beneath the reddish hair and over the closed eyes. I remember clearly how my wife and I talked about that afterward, when we got home from the Rosenfelds. It occurs to me that only then, when both of them were sitting with their eyes closed and it appeared as if they were looking and listening with their foreheads, only then were they really looking with their true eyes, with the eyes that were hidden behind their foreheads. Because when an artist is particularly captivated by something, he looks and sees not only with his external eyes which are beneath his brow, but also with his inner eyes, behind his brow. Chaim Weinberg was also an artist in his own way.

I remember how, one time when I was reading Most's *Freiheit* to him, he got up from his seat and hobbled around the room with his hand on his forehead. "Do you hear?" he said to me animatedly, "I think that even if I were a cold oven, I would start burning from that fire. He pointed at the newspaper. "Come on, I want to hear it again. Read the article again. Then we'll both become better anarchists." Most was his god, and not only his but the god of almost all the Jewish anarchists in those days.

The articles of my future friend Moiseev were published in Most's *Frieheit,* under the name Leontieff. I liked those articles. They always seemed to me like revolutionary songs in prose, sung by a revolutionary poet with a youthful and unique quest. Those articles spoke to my heart, but Weinberg didn't like them. "I don't know," he once said to me, "certainly Comrade Most knows better than I what to publish, but if you were to ask me, I wouldn't print those articles in the *Freiheit* nor in *Fraye Arbeter Shtime.* We must not make room in our newspapers for trifles, not even the prettiest. Our papers are revolutionary. They should agitate and propagandize so clearly, that a child could understand what we want and what we need and why we are striving for a free, anarchist society! Evidently Comrade Leontieff, while writing his articles, has his mind more on writing nicer trifles than on disseminating our ideas in the right way. I mean, as clear as 'for Rachel, your younger daughter,' and with the proper passion!"[203]

I didn't agree with him about Leontieff's articles. I actually did sense a revolutionary spirit in them. By the way, all the other Jewish comrades in those days had the same opinion about the printed word. Every printed word in their newspapers had to agitate and propagandize. This doesn't mean that Weinberg couldn't enjoy a good story which was not direct propaganda. In the social democratic *Arbeter Tsaytung*, which he read every week, he read stories by famous European writers in translation. He read some of those stories two or three times with the greatest pleasure. However, he maintained that this was, as he expressed it, a sort of tasty dish people could enjoy, but that would never be able to make them sated and healthy, and give them the proper energy, the revolutionary energy, as would a poem by David Edelstadt, for example, or by Morris Winchevsky.

I liked to attend his debates with the social democrats. I particularly remember one such debate on the topic, "Is it the worse the better as the anarchists say, or the better the better as the social democrats say?" The social democrat attempted to show what a good and fine speaker he was, so he spoke a Germanized Yiddish and used the words *niemals* and *sondern* and *abwahl* and *tat*, and other such words that our Yiddish long ago sent back to the Germans. Thereby he got very impassioned and excited, and he shouted until he became so hoarse that no one could hear his closing words. And Weinberg answered him so calmly and with such a clear, wonderful Yiddish for those days, compared with the Germanized language of the other fellow!

"Never have pleasures and riches and the good life made any revolutions in the world," Weinberg said, "and certainly not social revolutions, but rather human pain, human suffering and troubles, and human hunger. Therefore, we anarchists say *the worse the better;* this will bring us even closer to the

revolution and the revolution to us; and therefore I also hold
Jay Gould and Carnegie and Rockefeller to be our best
comrades, because they and their thievery propel the
revolution to us and spur it on with fiery whips. Faster!
Faster!" And he concluded with a parable that was so
humorous that the audience, except for the social democrats,
deafened the local with laughter.

Thanks to this Weinberg, I did something then that I
certainly would never do today, namely, I gave a lecture about
the Greek philosophers —no more, no less! By the way, I believe
one can still find a published report on the success of that
lecture in the *Fraye Arbeter Shtime* of 1892. How could such a
miracle come to pass, that I, who was so far from the Greek
philosophers, should come to give a lecture about them?

It happened like this: I read Draper's *A History of the
Intellectual Development in Europe*, and I liked it so much that
I was always talking with Weinberg about it. One time, he said
to me that I had gotten him so interested in what I had told
him about this work that he was sorry he wasn't able to read
the book for himself, especially the part about the Greek
philosophers. And whereas he liked the way I had spoken to
him about it, he thought that I should give a lecture about this
for the comrades and others. And my protestations that I was
not competent enough to give such a lecture were to no avail:
he stuck to his position. When one has even one drop of
knowledge that others in the masses do not have, one must
share it with them, he asserted. And thus the miracle came to
pass that I gave a lecture on the Greek philosophers and,
remarkably, both the lecturer and his lecture were well
received by the local! I don't think so just because a report to
that effect was subsequently published in the *Fraye Arbeter
Shtime,* but more so because among those who debated me at
the lecture, there was one, also an anarchist, a real Doctor of
Philosophy with the title Ph.D., a fellow by the name of
Hartmann,[204] a young man with red hair, as I recall, and he
debated with me as with someone who was a great expert in
Greek philosophy!

Something occurs to me now, that I have wondered about many times: the majority of our speakers gave such lectures, on other topics, as I gave mine. That is, they read a book, sometimes even a pamphlet, and then gave lectures about it before a large audience. It's true that for the scholar and the well-educated person, these lectures were not real lectures, but rather ignorance and perhaps worse than that. But those such as Weinberg, who understood these masses well and were themselves part of these masses, thought otherwise. With even one drop of knowledge more than the masses, we must share it with them –that was his opinion. I think that perhaps he was right: maybe one couldn't approach these Jewish masses except with a "drop of knowledge" in order to have an influence on them. Such lecturers as a Dr. Chaim Zhitlovsky or a Yitschak Isaac Hourwich, with their great knowledge, would certainly not have had any listeners among the Jewish masses in those days. After all, When Yitschak Isaac Hourwich wanted to give one of his proper lectures in those days, he had to travel to Chicago and give it in the university there!

At that time, Weinberg forbade me to see Boris and Anyuta, as well as the other friends I met with from time to time in Philadelphia. Even at those moments when I longed for my home in Vitebsk and my dear ones, I also ran to him. With him, I was able to forget about it. And one time, when he found out about my homesickness, he made fun of me. He laughed at me and said that when I came to America, I should have brought my mama's apron with me. Also at that time, the famous strike in Homestead (a town near Pittsburgh) took place in Carnegie's Steel and Iron Works. The strikers fought with weapons in their hands against hundreds of scabs, who were Pinkerton detectives. This particular strike bore the traits of a real war: there were dead and wounded on both sides. But the workers were victorious. The scab detectives had to capitulate. Then the anarchists were, of course, certain that the social revolution had begun, and two of them went to Homestead to the militant workers with a manifesto by Johann Most stating that they shouldn't be satisfied with their victory over scabs (over the Pinkertons, that is) but rather they should begin an armed struggle for the rights of all people. And then those same workers from Homestead, who had just recently fought with weapons in their hands against the scabs, nearly lynched the two anarchist guests who brought Most's manifesto. By some miracle, really, both of the messengers escaped town with their lives.

This was shortly before Alexander Berkman fired at Frick, the partner and principal manager of Carnegie's Steel and Iron Works.[205] I remember how Weinberg reacted to that. While all of us thought that this Homestead Strike, which had the whole country astir, was the social revolution, and Johann Most himself wrote more or less the same in *Freiheit*, Wenberg remained more calm than ever. He spoke calmly and coolly to me and to the others; he didn't get overly excited.

"It is for times like these," he said, "that people were given sense and reason. Certainly some spark has been ignited in our darkness, but perhaps not more than a straw roof, which the capitalist firefighters will quickly extinguish. We must wait: when the right roofs in Pittsburgh, Chicago, New York, and in Philadelphia start burning, then we'll know that this is the right fire!"

Later, when these same Homestead strikers treated the two anarchist messengers so badly, and when the anarchists –even Most himself –were so upset and embittered toward the Homestead workers because of that, Weinberg remained philosophical and tranquil then as well. He calmly said, "This only shows how much work we still have to do; how much darkness we still have to sweep from the minds of the masses!"

I don't know why he was so attached to me in those days, but he was fond of me, and he made a strong effort to keep me with the anarchists. He once said to me, "The misfortune with people like you is that at first, you burn so brightly that you burn out quickly. I'm afraid that in the end, you will follow your former friend Simon, and you too will start thinking about going to college, and if you study and become a doctor, you'll only be concerned with the masses as far as seeing if they bring a patient with a dollar for you." But he was seldom so hard on me. I heard mostly other words from him, kind and sincere words, full of praises for my devotion to the anarchist ideal. I don't have to yearn for my home and my dear ones, he pointed out to me. I should know that he and all the others also had a home, and also had a father and mother and brothers and sisters. And he also told me that I could become a speaker and a writer who would greatly benefit the masses. I just had to become better acquainted with anarchist communism, and instead of thinking about writing a "trifle with a sunrise" which might be appropriate to print in the social-democratic *ArbeiterZeitung,* better I should endeavor to compose something about the real "valley of lamentation" which could be printed in *Fraye Arbeter Shtime.*

In those days I read to him almost every sketch that I wrote in Russian, and although he couldn't read Russian at all, he could understand what I read to him. Just as he understood when I read him Most's *Freiheit* when he couldn't read German by himself at all. He once said to me that he had a good translator for one of my Russian sketches. It was a cigar maker who worked in the shop with him. This fellow had already translated something for the *Fraye Arbeter Shtime.* Therefore, I should endeavor to write something good. I promised him that I would.

Endnotes

Introduction

[1] See E. D. Cope, "On the Material Relations of Sex in Human Society," *The Monist*, Oct. 1890; De Cleyre's reply to his lecture at Ladies' Liberal League (Fall 1893) on that subject in *Lucifer the Light-Bearer* (Topeka, KS), April 20-May 11, 1894. On Brinton, see Memorial Address by Albert H. Smyth, *Proceedings of the American Philosophical Society*, January 16, 1900, last page; also de Cleyre, "Why I am an Anarchist," *Mother Earth*, March 1908, page 17; For Mt. Sinai Dispensary see Robert Helms, "Anarchists in Medicine and Pharmacy: Philadelphia, 1889-1930" *Clamor Magazine*, Dec. 2000/Jan. 2001.

[2] For the printed reaction against anarchists of the period, see Nhat Hong, *The Anarchist Beast: The Anti-Anarchist Crusade in Periodical Literature, 1884-1906;* Haymarket Press, Soil of Liberty pamphlet #3, Minneapolis (n.d. [c. 1975])

[3] Goldman, *Living My Life*, pp. 41-107, 413.

[4] Goldman, *Living My Life*, p. 157.

Original Introduction

[5] Weinberg Book Committee, Los Angeles, Radical Library, Branch 273 Workmen's Circle, Philadelphia.

[6] The Weinbergs appear on Abington Township land records as the owners of a parcel measuring 350 x 156 feet. The existing house at 3020 Old Welsh Road is almost certainly the house they lived in. However, they are listed as the owners from 1937 through 1941 only, while they lived there almost continuously from 1911 onward. We suspect that, since earlier records are lacking, the 1937 document was simply and updated deed. The site was a short walk from the Willow Grove Amusement Park, and was easily accessible from the city by trolley car. Weinberg's friend and fellow anarchist Walter "Vasya" Swieda lived nearby during the 1920's. See Avrich, *Anarchist Voices*, p. 370.

[7] Marcus Graham (1893-1985) was born Shmuel Marcus in Rumania and came to Philadelphia at age 14, becoming active in the Radical Library Group. During his career, Graham edited the journals *Anarchist Soviet Bulletin*, and *Free Society* in New York, then *MAN!* in San Francisco. After many years of government persecution, he went into hiding for

decades, communicating with anarchists again and writing during the 1970's. He was a proponent of propaganda by deed, including acts of terrorism and assassination. Graham was eccentric and personally unpopular. At the Ferrer Colony at Stelton NJ in the early 1930's, Sam Dolgoff recalled the he "was always spoiling for a fight... a terrible scandal-monger," who "always went barefoot, ate raw food, mostly nuts and raisins, and refused to use a tractor, being opposed to machinery. He didn't want to abuse horses, so he dug the earth himself." See Avrich, *Anarchist Voices*, pp. 421, 423, 488-89.

[8] Thomas B. Eyges (born around 1874) was a Russian-born Jew and lifelong anarchist. His memoir *Beyond the Horizon* was published in 1944, playfully reversing his name, i.e. narrating the life of "Mot Segye." Eyges emigrated to London in 1889 and to the USA in 1902.

[9] Weinberg's name appears on a short "Roster of Honor" among those who "did their share and more," on the last printed page of Elden LaMar, *The Clothing Workers of Philadelphia: History of Their Struggles for Union Security* (Philadelphia, 1940).

[10] "Did their own thing" (tr.).

[11] This was the period during which Eyges made his living as a traveling salesman.

[12] A prayer shawl (tr.).

[13] Fund-raising picnics were held many times at the Weinberg place, to benefit various anarchist newspapers. See, for example, *Challenge*, Aug. 27, 1937.

Chapter 1

[14] Weinberg's death record Montgomery County PA, January 28, 1939, #8815, gives his parents' names as Isar (or perhaps Isac) Weinberg and Sophie Faga Weinberg.

[15] A gymnasium was a secondary school. (tr.)

[16] Charles Bradlaugh (1833-1891) was the famous atheist leader who was elected to the British Parliament in 1880.

[17] The modern spelling convention is Ciechanowiec. Variously listed as being in Lomza Province or in Bialystok District, the town was part of the Russian Empire when Weinberg was a boy, and is now in Poland.

[18] The ship *Italy* sailed from Liverpool to New York, arriving on October 17, 1881, listing "Weinberg, Ch.," age 20, among its passengers. See

Glazier, Ira A., editor, *Migration from the Russian Empire: Lists of Passengers Arriving at the Port of New York; Vol. 1* (1975), pp. 360-61.

[19] From 1881 till early 1884, James Buchanan "Buck" Duke of the W. Duke & Sons Tobacco Company arranged for skilled rollers to be hired in New York, and sent to Durham to work. These included former employees of the Goodwin Tobacco Company who had been striking there. This episode was the origin of the Jewish community of Durham, and is described at length by Leonard Rogoff in *Homelands: Jewish Identity in Durham and Chapel Hill, North Carolina* (University of Alabama Press, 2001), chapter 4. Weinberg, apparently, was recruited late in this period.

[20] Bernhard Goldgar was a Polish Jew who had already been active in the New York Jewish Socialist movement. Always considering himself an anarchist, he became active in the Jewish community and even president of a synagogue. He eventually settled in Macon, Georgia. See Elias Tcherikower, ed., *The Early Jewish Labor Movement in the United States*, revised edition (1961); p. 206. Goldgar, who was in his early twenties when he met Weinberg, left an unpublished memoir, which relates his conversion from pious Judaism to revolutionary ideas after – not before – his arrival in the United States. See Rogoff, *Homelands,* pp. 40-42, 325, n. 5.

[21] Johann Joseph Most (1846-1906) arrived in the United States in December of 1882, and seems to be the "famous social-anarchist" who inspired Goldgar's conversion, as mentioned in Rogoff, p. 42. The earliest surviving Yiddish translations of the pamphlets *Property Beast* and *God Pestilence* were published in 1888, translated by Benj. Feigenbaum and J. Jaffa, respectively. Weinberg may have read an earlier translation, since he met Goldgar no later than 1884. See J. Patten (ed.), *The Yiddish Anarchist Bibliography* (1998). The best discussion of Most's career in English – not nearly as flattering as Weinberg's – is *Gemeinschaft and Revolution: The German Anarchist Movement in New York City, 1880-1914* by Tom Goyens, PhD Diss., K.U. Leuven, Germany (2003).

[22] The German-Jewish poet Heinrich Heine (1797-1856) was sometimes translated and published in anarchist periodicals during Weinberg's lifetime.

[23] The Bonsack cigarrette rolling and cutting machine was first installed at the Duke factory on April 30, 1884. See Rogoff, p. 42.

[24] There actually was a Local Chapter 27 of the Cigarmakers' Progressive Union from July 1884, and Bernhard Goldgar was one of its officers. See Rogoff, p. 43.

[25] Alexander Jonas (1834-1912) was the first editor of the Socialist daily *New Yorker Volkszeitung*, which began publication in January, 1878. See Tcherikower, ed., *The Early Jewish Labor Movement*, etc; p. 88.

[26] Among his many dramatic roles, Most starred as Baumert in *Die Weber* (The Weavers) in New York during the Fall season of 1894 and again, at the Thalia Theater at 46 Bowery, in 1904.   See *Liberty*, December 1, 1894 and Emma Goldman, *Living My Life*, p. 380.

[27] Most's last public appearance was his 60th birthday celebration in Philadelphia on March 10, 1906 where he caught a bad cold, then traveled to Cincinnati and died on March 17th. Weinberg, apparently, was not present at the birthday party, which was disrupted by the police, at Equity Hall, 1024 Lombard Street. See *Public Ledger*, March 11, 1906.

[28] For The Yom Kippur Ball of October 1889, Most spoke at the Fourth Street Labor Lyceum in Manhattan. This probably is the occasion Weinberg refers to. See Paul Avrich, *Anarchist Portraits*, p. 181; Tcherikower, ed., *The Early Jewish Labor Movement,* etc; pp. 259-261.

[29] He means Blackwell's Island Penitentiary, which was on what is now called Roosevelt Island, in the East River.

[30] Mikhail Aleksandrovich Bakunin (1814-1876) was the founder of the modern anarchist movement. He was directly involved the abortive Dresden uprising of 1848, and influenced other revolutionary struggles.

Chapter 2

[31] The 1930 City Directory lists Bayuk Bros. Cigars, NW corner 9th Street and Columbia Ave., Philadelphia. The company was started by Samuel, Meyer, and Max Bayuk, sons of Moyshe (Moses) Bayuk (1850-1932), an "assimilated, secularly educated lawyer, greatly inspired by Tolstoy." He was a leading member of the Alliance Colony and served as justice of the Peace in the area. Jacob (Jack) Bayuk was Moyshe's oldest son. See *A Farmer's Daughter* by Bluma Bayuk Rappaport Purmell (Moyshe's daughter) and Ellen Eisenberg, *Jewish Agricultural Colonies in New Jersey, 1882-1920* (Syracuse University Press 1995). In the

Yiddish edition, the name Bayuk was misspelled as "Burke" or "Bourke," apparently misunderstood by Marcus Graham.

[32] Carmel, New Jersey is a small town in Cumberland County, about 30 miles due south of Philadelphia. It was started in 1882 as a Jewish agricultural colony, part of the Am Olam movement. Carmel was organized and financed by the radical-leaning scholar Michael Heilprin (actually a Polish Jew), and his Montefiore Agricultural Aid Society. There were, however, other Am Olam colonies nearby that were financed by the (German-Jewish) Hebrew Immigrant Aid Society. Before 1882 Carmel had already been occupied by German-Jewish families from Philadelphia who tried unsuccessfully at farming. See *Jewish Exponent*, Nov. 1, 1889; Ellen Eisenberg, *Jewish Agricultural Colonies* (1995), pp. 106-115.

[33] Braided Sabbath loaves (tr).

[34]John Mahlon Barnes (1866-1934) was a key figure in the Cigar Makers International Union and a longtime opponent of Samuel Gompers. He became a key figure in the Pennsylvania Labor scene, and ran for governor on the Socialist ticket. See his obituary in *New York Times* Feb. 23, 1934, p. 22; also, Barnes is mentioned profusely in J. Robert Constantine ed.), *Letters of Eugene V. Debs, Vol. 1 1874-1912*, University of Illinois Press, 1990. See also Gary M. Fink et al, (eds.) *Biographical Dictionary of American Labor Leaders*, Greenwood Press, 1974.

[35] We have evidence of only four years in the life of "Professor" Thomas Hamilton Garside. A native of Scotland (or Northern England), he was listed in Baltimore's city directory as a Reverend for the Mt. Winans Methodist Episcopal Church (1888) and then as an insurance agent (1889 & 1890). Levine states that he was a lecturer for the Knights of Labor and the director of a private school in Philadelphia. His duplicitous conduct in the Cloakmakers' strike of 1890 raised suspicions. During 1889-90 he gave public lectures in Philadelphia, and became the (opportunistic) lover of the young Voltairine de Cleyre for a short time. At this juncture he was lecturing on "what to do with the children," developing a reputation as a "professional seducer of women," and writing for the Philadelphia *Times*. In June 1891, the front pages of Philadelphia's dailies exposed, in minute detail, Garside not only as a Deputy U.S. Marshall, but one who embarrassed the Marshall's office by inventing heroic stories about chasing a banker-turned-embezzler, and

injuries as well. He went to his residence on 8th Street in Camden accompanied by a woman, and from there he vanishes from history. See *Times, Press, Record,* June 21-25, *NY Times,* June 21-23, 1891; *Twentieth Century,* Feb 13, 1890, July 2, 1891; Levine, *Women's Garment Workers,* pp. 50-53, 584; and Avrich, *An American Anarchist,* pp. 51-53.

[36] Joseph Barondess (1867-1928), born in Russia, came from an Orthodox Jewish background and went to England as a youth, arrived in the US in 1888, having already become a trade unionist. He studied law and became a leading organizer among the garment workers of New York. Barondess led the important Cloakmakers' Strike of 1890, which involved many anarchist organizers, but his leadership badly weakened the union. Known for his impetuous and divisive personality, he later became a Zionist. See, for example, Fink et al, *Biographical Dictionary,* etc., 1974, pp. 15-16; Louis Levine, *The Women's Garment Workers: A History of the International Ladies' Garment Workers' Union* (New York, 1924) pp. 58-64. Bernard Braff was a cloakmaker, active unionist 1890-1904, and later in business. See again Levine, page 582.

[37] M. Kuntz was the secretary of the Operators' and Cloakmakers' Union No. 1 from 1890-93. See Levine, *Women's Garment Workers,* p. 587.

[38] One is not sure whether this is meant ironically; it would depend on how poor they were and the size of the herring (tr.).

Chapter 3

[39] This was the Turgeniev Debating Club, founded October 1887. See Herz Burgin, *Di geshikhte fun der yidisher arbeter bavegung in Amerike, Rusland, un England* (New York, 1915), p 173.

[40] According to Tcherikower, this is "evidently David Goldstein," (b. 1868) the proletarian poet. See Elias Tcherikower, ed., *The Early Jewish Labor Movement,* etc., pp. 223, 226.

[41] The 1890 City Directory reads: Morris Rittenberg, Tailor, home 240 Catherine Street. *Freiheit,* 22 June 1889 lists Marie Rittenberg as the secretary of the Knights of Liberty.

[42] E. Gretch (sometimes Gratz) had the title Professor in news accounts of a speech he made alongside Weinberg on June 19, 1891, during a strike against the sweating system. See *Times,* "Tailors in Mass Meeting" and *Philadelphia Inquirer,* "They're Bound to Win," June 20.

[43] The original reads "the New York group Knights of Liberty," but that name was used only for the Philadelphia group. All the others were Pioneers.

[44] Isidore Solomon Prenner (born c.1867) – often spelled Brenner – emigrated from Russia in 1885. Apart from the scenes Weinberg relates in chapter 13, Prenner appears again after the "Broad Street Riot," speaking out in Philadelphia against anarchism and atheism. See *Philadelphia Record*, Feb. 24, 1908. Records regarding this man are generally lacking and not always perfectly consistent, but the 1930 Federal Population Census seems to find him living alone in a rented room at Washington D.C.

[45] Jacob Abraham Maryson (1866-1941) was a frequent contributor (sometimes as "F. A. Frank") and editor in the Yiddish anarchist press, and he translated many anarchist texts into that language. He authored books including *The Theory and Practice of Anarchism* (1927).

[46] This may be "Y. Weinberg from Atlantic City," the same comrade he will mention in Chapter 13.

[47] Michael A. Cohn (1867-1939), the Jewish, Russian-born New York cardiologist, was a devoted anarchist throughout his life: in 1890 he and Annie Netter led an anti-religious meeting in Baltimore, suffering beating and police harassment: in 1918 he posted bail for anarchists accused of sedition; in the 1920's he funded and wrote for *The Road to Freedom,* and fought on behalf of the condemned anarchists Sacco and Vanzetti; in 1936 he delivered a eulogy for his comrade Alexander Berkman. Dr. Cohn treated poor anarchists for free when they were unable to pay. See Paul Avrich, *Anarchist Voices* (Princeton, 1995), pp. 329, 433; Richard Polenberg, *Fighting Faiths* (New York, 1987); Philadelphia *Evening Bulletin*, Sept. 29, 1890

[48] We know little about the anarchist Hermann Strumpen, sometimes of Philadelphia, but this is probably who Weinberg means. He was active by October 1883, when he represented Philadelphia area branches at the convention of International Working People's Association at Pittsburgh. We last spot him in '89, when he served as secretary of the Progressive Arbeiterbund of Philadelphia. (see *Freiheit*, Oct. 20, 1883 & June 22, 1889). In the short-lived *Die Zukunft*, 10 May 1884, Strumpen, a follower of Most, has an advertisement offering his services as a fire-insurance agent, covering furniture to $500. This leads us to suspect, while yet unable to prove, that he was linked to the "firebug" scandal,

which exposed the fact that several New York anarchists close to Most had been torching insured apartments to raise money for the movement. For the early end of the thread, see "The Beast of Communism," *Liberty,* Mar. 27, 1886. At least one of the known fires caused deaths among nearby tenants.

[49] Samuel H. Gordon, MD (1871-1906) came from his native Russia in 1890 and immediately got involved in the labor struggle at Philadelphia, being arrested on Aug. 4, 1890 during the cloak makers' strike for "riotous conduct." Working as a cigar roller, he graduated from Medico-Chirurgical College (Philadelphia) in 1898, setting up his practice at 531 Pine Street. He lectured on revolutionary anarchism in radical clubs, but he is remembered mostly for his stormy 6-year romance with Voltairine de Cleyre, who taught him English and financed his education. Together the available information creates an unflattering image of Gordon. He left the anarchist movement by 1899, removed to Newark, NJ in 1904 and died there of "acute gastritis" at age 36. See *AMA Directory of Deceased American Physicians* (1998); Glazier, Ira A., ed., *Migration from the Russian Empire,* etc., (1975), passenger list for the *Dania,* Mar. 31, 1890, p. 201; death notice in *Evening Bulletin* (Philadelphia) Nov. 11, 1906; "Strikers Beyond Bounds," *Press,* Aug 5, 1890.

[50] Max Barbour, MD (born 1875) was a pantsmaker, then graduated from Medico-Chirurgical College of Philadelphia 1898 (a classmate of Samuel Gordon's). Leon Kobrin mentioned in 1942 that Barbour had one eye (see appendix).

[51] Dr. Max Staller (1868-1919) and his wife, Jennie Magul Staller (1872-1957) were involved in the anarchist movement from the early 1890's until around 1905. Both born in Galicia (now in Austria), they were members of an amateur theatrical company called the Star Specialty Club for some years (incl. 1891). Dr. Staller earned his M.D. at the University of Illinois in 1895, and quickly earned great distinction in the profession at Philadelphia. He was first President of the Mt. Sinai Dispensary at 236 Pine Street, which he organized in 1899 along with other anarchist-physicians. In 1910 he organized the Jewish Consumptive Institute at 406 Wharton, where he was a leading researcher on tuberculosis until his death from throat cancer in 1919. During his days in the Knights of Liberty he was called the "boy chieftain" and was considered "the best speaker on the Jewish street." See Harry D. Boonin, *The Jewish Quarter of Philadelphia: A History and Guide, 1881-1930* (Philadelphia, 1999),

p. 117-18; "Battle with Strikers," *Philadelphia Times*, August 4, 1890; "Theater Shtik," (event notice) *Fraye Arbeter Shtime*, March 27, 1891; Obituary, *Philadelphia Evening Bulletin,* March 22, 1919.

[52] Louis (Bandes) Miller, an immigrant Jew from Vilna, was editor of the Russian socialist newspaper *Znamia* in 1890, and remained one of the most influential immigrant Jewish intellectuals. He also edited the *Jewish Daily Warheit* from 1910-17. Morris (Hillkowitz) Hillquit (1869-1933) was a major figure in the American socialist movement, and had a long career as a journalist in the Yiddish press. The famous Abraham Cahan, (1860-1951) later the editor of the *Forverts* (Forward), was one of the most influential of Jewish socialists. Michael Zametkin (1859-1935) was a primarily Russian-speaking Jewish immigrant who arrived from Odessa in 1882. He and his wife Adela Kean Zametkin mastered Yiddish in the United States and earned their living as journalists in that language. Benjamin Feigenbaum (b. 1860) was a master of anti-religious satire, the son of Hasidic parents in Warsaw, Poland. After rejecting the religion, he emigrated to Belgium, then to London, and finally in 1891 to New York. A celebrated atheist speaker and writer, Feigenbaum was an organizer of the "Yom Kippur Balls" in both London and New York. See Steven Cassedy, *To the Other Shore: The Russian Jewish Intellectuals Who Came To America* (Princeton, 1997); Levine, *Women's Garment Workers*, p. 589.

[53] "Torah with common sense"

[54] We assume that Prenner led the original faction, while Gordon named the new group, because Prenner left the anarchist movement in 1892, while the "New Generation" group remains in Philadelphia about another six years, when Gordon, too, left. It is very possible that the meeting place at "Third and Gaskill" was at 512 South 3rd Street (a few doors above Gaskill), the same building in which the Stallers produced amateur plays and the Yom Kippur Ball meeting was raided (see Chapter 4).

Chapter 4

[55] The term "Yahudim" (Hebrew, meaning Jews), was used to refer to the Americanized Jews whose families had arrived from Central Europe in the mid-nineteenth century. This was in contrast with the poorer Eastern European "Yidn" (also meaning Jews, but the Yiddish word), who had arrived in large numbers after 1880 (tr).

[56] Isidore Prenner (see Chapter 3, note 3), Julius Moscowitz, Morris Gillis, and Louis Jacobson were arrested on the evening of October 11, 1891 for incitement to riot at a meeting at 512 South 3rd Street, 3rd floor. Jacob Appel was charged with intimidating a witness, but then released when the others were held for trial on October 16.

[57] He is referring to the important cloakmakers' strike of May 16- Aug. 23, 1890. The Blum Brothers (Isaac, Gabriel, & Ralph), 1319 Market Street, were prominent in the Philadelphia Cloak Manufacturers' Association, which included 35 firms. Max Staller (see Chapter 3, note 8) and Prenner were indeed the strike leaders, and Staller was arrested for allegedly inciting a riot during the strike. The Blum Brothers firm was first to bring in African-American women as strike-breakers. See Maxwell Whiteman, "The Cloakmakers Strike of 1890" in *Jewish Exponent*, October 16 & 23, 1964; also *Gopsill's City Directory*, 1891; *Philadelphia Times*, August 8, 1890; *Philadelphia Inquirer*, Aug. 16, 1890, and other contemporary newspaper accounts.

[58] A *khevre-kedisha* is a burial society. *Tefillin* are two small black leather boxes containing biblical verses inscribed on parchment, fastened with leather straps to the forehead and arm during morning prayers (tr).

[59] The present trial scene took place on March 18, 1892. The defense attorney named in news accounts was E. Clinton Rhoades.

[60] The Friendship Liberal League was established around 1873. The club had anarchist members from 1891 or earlier and still existed in 1959. In February 1892 several anarchist women left to form the Ladies' Liberal League, which became the city's main English venue for anarchists through at least 1898. The Friendship met at Broad & Wood Streets at the time of this trial, and Dr. John Kaye was its president. See *Fifteenth Annual Congress, American Secular Union, Held in Philadelphia, October 31, 1891* (Historical Society of Wisconsin, pamphlet collection, #50-108); Voltairine de Cleyre, "What women are doing in Philadelphia," *Lucifer the Light Bearer*, Aug. 31, 1894; de Cleyre, "The Past and Future of the Ladies' Liberal League," *The Rebel*, Oct. and Nov. 1895; and "A letter from Emma Goldman," *Solidarity*, March 15, 1898; *The Freethinker* (Philadelphia) Jan. 1959.

[61] Natasha Notkin (b. 1870) was born in Russia and became a nihilist before immigrating to the United States at the age of fifteen. The bobbed hairstyle described here was not uncommon among radical Russian women of the time. Around 1899 she began learning the pharmacy trade

from fellow anarchist Jacob L. Joffe, and became his business partner in a new drug store at 2630 East Lehigh Avenue. That store was listed in the City Directory from 1907-17. From 1899-1904, she was the Philadelphia agent for *Free Society*, and then from 1906-17 for *Mother Earth*, which were the leading English-language anarchist-communist papers of the era. A highly respected anarchist and a close confidant of both Voltairine de Cleyre and Emma Goldman, Notkin took pains to avoid taking credit for her substantial contribution to the movement. Indeed the present courtroom scene is one of two surviving brief passages of her own words that we have been able to locate. Sometimes called the "soul" of Philadelphia's anarchism, she organized an elaborate annual spring fund-raiser called the Russian Tea Party from 1897-1916. She is mentioned fondly by Goldman in *Living My Life*, pp. 123, 157, 196. See, in *Free Society*, "Among Ourselves" Apr. 12, 1903 and "A Little Journey" Sept. 20, 1903; also Federal Census Record for Philadelphia City, June 4, 1900 (residence 327 Pine Street).

[62] Hugh Owen Pentecost (1848-1907) had a long career as a protestant preacher from 1871 (Baptist, then Evangelical, then Congregational). He was involved in several pastoral conflicts, including when he was forced from his pastorate in Newark, NJ late in 1887, after passionately denouncing the execution of the Haymarket anarchists in his Sunday sermon. At that time he renounced Orthodox Christianity and instead made independent weekly sermons on social questions of the day and founded, then for 4 years edited *Twentieth Century*, a popular radical weekly in whose July 6, 1889 issue he stated that Jesus was "an Anarchistic-Communist." By then, Pentecost was in regular contact with Philadelphia anarchists. With his politics first anchoring to the Single Tax, and briefly to anarchism, he again changed in 1892, when he became an attorney and gave up his editorship. In December 1893, Pentecost accepted an appointment as assistant district attorney in Manhattan, which precipitated a renunciation of his radical views. After a public outcry about his radicalism, the appointment was canceled anyway. Although he continued with an impressive career as a criminal lawyer (even addressing the US Supreme Court in 1898), he never regained the respect of many anarchists. From the early '90's he was also an active Freethinker, advocating the strict separation of religion from all civic affairs. Although Pentecost defended the Yom Kippur defendants in print and was involved in Brooklyn as a speaker (1890), and may have

been present at these proceedings, he was not admitted to the Bar until nine months later – in New York, not Pennsylvania – and he did not formally represent them (the defense counsel was E. Clinton Rhoads). Pentecost helped many anarchists over the years, either as counsel or as an advisor when they faced criminal charges, and was known as a defender of Free Speech and a brilliant public speaker. For the radical version of his life, see *Twentieth Century,* Dec. 3, 1891; Voltairine de Cleyre, "Hugh O. Pentecost," in *Mother Earth*, March 1907; Jonathan Mayo Crane, "In Memory of Hugh O. Pentecost," in *Lucifer*, February 14, 1907. For his views on the Yom Kippur balls, see "The Brooklyn Outrage" in *Twentieth Century*, October 9, 1890. See also *New York Times*, Oct. 17, 1880 and Dec. 12, 1887; Colgate University, Alumni Archives.

[63] Prenner seems to have been among the very earliest students at The Temple College (later Temple University; established informally in 1884; chartered 1888), but the records of the first few years are woefully incomplete. It is possible that Weinberg is confusing Central High School with Temple. In either case we cannot determine who the professor was or what Prenner studied. Some sources have him going to Chicago after his release, but details are lacking.

[64] An unsigned letter to the anarchist paper *Solidarity* (New York), November 5, 1892, describes Prenner's proposals, made shortly after his release, with disappointment: he wanted the anarchists to make peace with Social Democrats and endorse their electoral candidates. The writer regarded the proposal as a "compromise" that would be a "pure loss" for the anarchists.

Chapter 5

[65] The meaning of a miserable fifth is unclear, but may mean a fifth of a dollar per hour (tr.).

[66] Voltairine de Cleyre reported in *Free Society*, August 18, 1901 that the Jewish Workers' Cooperative Association, "initiated and very largely organized by" Weinberg, had "something like nine hundred members," had been holding "crowded meetings, weekly, all winter," and that it had already opened a shoe store.

[67] We have not determined the dates of these early meetings, but if Emma Goldman addressed one of them, it would have been after

December 1900, when she returned from a 13-month stay in England. Her last known lectures in Philadelphia before that trip took place February 8-19, 1899; she returned to the city again April 7-20, 1901.

[68] The City Directory for 1901 lists the cigar maker Meyer Gillis, residing at 814 Reed Street. Just after the shooting of President McKinley, when all anarchists were under police surveillance, The Cooperative Association was prohibited from meeting at Washington Hall (525 South 4th St.), and Gillis, its President, was quoted in news accounts, saying that the police order was unfair. See "Police Begin War on Anarchists," *Press,* Sept. 15. 1901

[69] During the late 1890's, A. L. Wolfson contributed revolutionary poems to the London anarchist paper *Der Arbeter Fraynd*, which were popular on both sides of the Atlantic. See William J. Fishman, *East End Jewish Radicals, 1875-1914*, p. 223.

[70] The slogans were carried on banners or placards (tr).

[71] The tailors Harris and Louis Gersten, who lived at 726 Sears St., were the only Gerstens in the 1901 City Directory.

[72] A. G. Margolin was a lawyer who spoke in the Philadelphia's radical clubs around the turn of the century. His lecture topics included Socialism and "Evolution of the Family."

[73] Max Barbour, M.D. (See Chapter 3, note 9).

Chapter 6

[74] This is the same Dr. Michael A. Cohn as is mentioned in Chapter 3.

[75] Harry Gordon (1866-1941) was a leading anarchist in Pittsburgh for many years. He was nearly lynched by vigilantes (see Chapter 15) and arrested following the shooting of President McKinley in September 1901 on suspicion of having a connection to the crime, but was soon released.

[76] Probably Max Kisliuk of Atlantic City, whose daughter Lilly Dinowitzer became an active anarchist in Washington D.C.. See Avrich, *Anarchist Voices*, p. 208.

[77] Jacob Gordin (1853-1909), the great Ukranian-born Yiddish playwright, was described by the contemporary playwright Leon Kobrin as "Straight as a palm, his stately beard solemnly covering his wide chest, his eyes like two points of fire, sharp as daggers. In his right hand he carries a cane; in his left, one of his plays. He is going to the theater to

read it to the actors. People who know him say, 'that is Jacob Gordin.' Those who do not know him stop and remark, 'what a fine man!'" See Ronald Sanders, *The Downtown Jews: Portrait of an Immigrant Generation* (New York, 1969).

[78] This places the scene a few years prior to October 7, 1899. On that date, the depressed and physically ill "M. Levitsky" hanged himself at his home in San Francisco, where he had moved a year earlier. He was well liked by other anarchists, who were badly offended when the *Morning Call* ran a sensational, disrespectful report of his death. See *Free Society*, Oct. 15 & 22, 1899.

[79] "S. Bookbinder" was an active anarchist of Providence, and raised a defense fund when his local comrade John H. Cook (1851-1931) was jailed for strike support activity in the fall of 1902. See *Free Society*, Nov. 23, 1902.

[80]   David Edelstadt (1866-1892) was born in Kaluga, Russia, and published Russian poems by age eleven. He was already politicized by May of 1881, when he lived in Kiev and was wounded in the pogrom, which galvanized his Jewish identity. He joined the Kiev *Am Olam,* and at age 16 immigrated to Cincinnati. Converting to anarchism after the Haymarket executions of 1887, he started his short but brilliant career as one of the four Yiddish "sweatshop poets." He was also an early editor of the *Fraye Arbeter Shtime.* He died of tuberculosis after moving to Denver in an attempt to slow the progress of the disease. He was so loved for his poems (songs) that there were anarchist Edelstadt singing clubs in many U.S. cities for over sixty years after he died. One verse of Edelstadt's was translated as follows: *How long, Oh how long shall your strength be sold/ And a whip hang over your head?/ How long shall you build cities of gold/ For those who are stealing your bread?* See Philip S Foner (ed), *American labor Songs of the Nineteenth Century,* (Urbana, IL 1975); pp. 230, 315, 318-19; Aaron Kramer (ed/tr), *A Century of Yiddish Poetry,* (New York, 1989), pp. 59-62.

[81] Joseph J. Cohen recalled that Benny Moore, an older local anarchist, had told the story about Comrade Feitelson, who later went by Telson and was the brother-in law of David Edelstadt. Telson came to Philadelphia from Chicago and announced that "everything is in tip-top shape for the social revolution," and that when groups in other cities were as prepared as was his own group, the signal would be given and "revolution would encircle the whole country." The Philadelphia group

was not impressed. Joseph J. Cohen, *The Jewish Anarchist Movement in the United States*, (in Yiddish, Philadelphia 1945); chapter "Anarchist Movement in Philadelphia in the 1880's;" unpublished 1980 translation by Esther Dolgoff.

[82] De Cleyre's first tour of Britain was from June to October 1897. She gave successful lectures all over England and Scotland.

[83] L. Baron was an established London anarchist by 1894, when he served as co-editor of the *Arbeter Fraynd*. Discussions at the Sugar Loaf Pub anarchist meetings "often became heated, particularly between such two self-acknowledged depositors of wisdom as the able dialectician Kaplan and emotional rebel Baron." In 1905 Baron was part of a faction that raised a failed campaign of hatred against Rudolf Rocker among the Jewish anarchists of London. William J. Fishman, *East End Jewish Radicals* (Duckworth 1975), pp. 217-18, 220, 236, 274.

[84] We have no information about this son, nor do we know who the mother was. See Chapter 15 for further discussion.

[85] Born in Lithuania, I. (Yud) Kaplan discovered a gift for oratory early in his life. He emigrated to Leeds, England, where he worked as a machinist and became both anarchist and atheist. Although not well educated, he was considered a fine intellectual and was a very popular speaker in London's East End during and after the 1890's. In 1912 Kaplan was secretary of the London Ladies' Tailors' Union. See William J. Fishman, *East End Jewish Radicals, 1875-1914* p. 242, 294-95.

[86] Moritz Jaeger was an anarchist of London's East End who moved to Liverpool, where he established a print shop. There, in 1898, he persuaded Rudolf Rocker to edit the short-lived Yiddish weekly *Dos Fraye Vort*, which began Rocker's distinguished career as the non-Jewish editor of Yiddish anarchist papers. Jaeger married the anarchist Fanny Weinberg. See Fishman, *East End Jewish Radicals*, pp. 220, 222, 239.

[87] Abraham Frumkin (1873-1940) was a major intellectual of the Jewish anarchist movement, but he has been largely forgotten. Born in Jerusalem, he spent parts of his life in Constantinople, England, Paris, and New York. He was literate in several languages and translated dozens of anarchist books into Yiddish. He wrote for various anarchist papers, particularly the *Arbeter Fraynd* in London.

[88] Peter Kropotkin (1842-1921) stands preeminent among all the anarchists in the history of the movement. Born in Russia to a wealthy,

aristocratic family with the title "Prince," he renounced the title and devoted his long and brave life to the anarchist cause. The leading intellectual of Anarchist Communism, he was respected by, but never aligned with Johann Most, who inspired Weinberg. His many books include *The Conquest of Bread* and *Mutual Aid: A Factor in Evolution.* In October 1897 he visited Philadelphia for one lecture, where the Social Science Club published his pamphlet *Modern Science and Anarchism* (translated by its member David A. Modell, a young teacher) in 1903.

[89] John Turner (1864-1934) was active in the (anarchist) Freedom group in London, and was the general secretary of the Shop Assistants' Union, which he organized in the mid-1890's. He had already lectured in Philadelphia in 1896, and he would become famous in 1903-04, when he was the first foreign anarchist to be deported under the anti-anarchist law enacted after McKinley's assassination.

[90] V. N. Cherkezov (1846-1925) was a Georgian anarchist writer of high birth and an associate of Peter Kropotkin's in England. He had attended a welcoming tea for Voltairine de Cleyre during her 1897 visit to London.

Chapter 7

[91] Voltairine de Cleyre (Nov. 17, 1866-June 20, 1912) was an anarchist whose writings, charismatic personality, and dedication inspired many people. She was educated at the Convent of Our Lady of Lake Huron in Sarnia, Ontario between the ages of thirteen and seventeen, but she did not become a nun. After moving to Philadelphia in 1889, she gave private lessons in English, French, mathematics, and piano to make her living. De Cleyre was an activist, essayist, and poet with an international reputation. See Paul Avrich, *An American Anarchist: The Life of Voltairine de Cleyre* (Princeton, 1978).

[92] Herman Helcher had taken English lessons from Voltairine, but she had not seen him for two years prior to his attack. See *North American* (Philadelphia), Dec. 23, 1902.

[93] Weinberg's friendship with de Cleyre was not as close as he suggests here (although they held a high regard for each other as comrades), as we see by his clearly mistaken version of this episode. She did indeed love Nathan Navro as a very close friend, but it is very unlikely that they ever became lovers even briefly, since there is nowhere any suggestion to that

effect. When the shooting occurred, she lived with her comrades George Brown and Mary Hansen at 807 Fairmount Avenue, and not with Navro, who did, however, rent a room in the house where she recovered from illness in 1905. In de Cleyre's letters, she refers to Weinberg only by his surname, whereas she calls closer friends (such as Navro, Hansen, and Brown) by their first names or by affectionate nicknames. Indeed Voltairine's son detested Weinberg, once writing that "Weinberg was so conceited and so fond of the limelight that he would strut and seek the reflected glory of association with my mother whenever possible." See letter, Harry de Cleyre to Agnes Inglis, Feb. 15, 1948 (Labadie Collection).

[94] By all accounts, Helcher stalked his prey before the shooting, but Weinberg's statement that he rented a room across the street has no second. Also, Voltairine was getting onto, not off of, the streetcar.

[95] The shooting occurred at 2 p.m. on December 19, 1902. Actually, de Cleyre was struck by three bullets, and spent about three weeks in Hahnemann Hospital.

[96] The effort to save the deranged comrade from harsh punishment began soon after the shooting. In spite of the efforts of the anarchists, who paid two lawyers to represent him, he was sentenced to six years and nine months in prison, but was soon transferred to the state mental hospital at Norristown, PA.

[97] John Wanamaker (1838-1922) made his fortune in department stores, and served as U.S. Postmaster General (1889-93). The English-language radical press criticized Wanamaker for his censorship of literature (assisting the ruthless anti-vice crusader Anthony Comstock), for his anti-union business practices, and for just as corrupt in politics as those he publicly denounced as a reform leader. In 1889, he ordered the arrest of W. E. Reid for mailing a spiritualist newspaper. In 1890, Wanamaker banned Tolstoy's newly-translated *Kreutzer Sonata* from the mails after asking for, but not getting, a special discount price from the publisher (the anarchist Benjamin R. Tucker) for his own store. In 1898, the Philadelphia anarchist John A. Wilson wrote that he had earlier served two years in prison for mailing an "obscene" book that was on sale at Wanamaker's store at the same time. "Pious John," as he was called, had two daughters, Mary and Elizabeth. See *Truth Seeker*, Aug. 3, 1889 (editorial); *Boston Globe*, Aug. 1, 1890; "Wanamaker's latest crime"

Liberty, Aug. 16, 1890; *Free Society*, Jan. 16, 1898; "Political Career of John Wanamaker," *Justice* (Wilmington, DE) Feb. 19, 1898, p. 1.

[98] Possibly David Cohen, of 1724 South 6th Street, who was arrested in the "Broad Street Riot" affair of 1908 along with Weinberg and de Cleyre, but quickly released. See *North American*, Feb. 22, 1908.

[99] This is a professional portrait of de Cleyre, taken in 1901 by Henry Bridle, at his studio at 913 Arch Street. She also knew Bridle as a theosophist. See Voltairine de Cleyre to Harriet De Claire, July 25, 1901, Labadie Collection.

[100] William Charles Owen (1854-1929) edited the English section of *Regeneración* from 1911 until 1916, when the Magon brothers were arrested on February 18, and Owen was also sought by the authorities. He eluded capture and fled to England, where he remained until his death in West Sussex. See Heiner Becker, "W. C. Owen," *Freedom: A Hundred Years October 1886 to October 1986* (London, 1986).

[101] This occasion was related by de Cleyre in a letter, wherein she mentions that Weinberg was in Chicago "waiting around to be sent back to Cleveland for the strike there, before going to California." See Voltairine de Cleyre to Joseph J. Cohen June 7, 1911, Cohen papers, YIVO Archive, New York.

[102] While his work as a labor activist was respected by all, Brown's opinions on morals were by no means popular among anarchist women. In 1903, his articles on "varietism" (non-monogamy) and prostitution precipitated blistering replies from several, including his own partner, Mary. See *Lucifer the Light-Bearer*, May 21, June 4, 17, & 25, July 23, Aug.13, and Dec. 17, 1903.

[103] George died on from an infection in his hand, resulting from a splinter. His condition was serious enough to be seen by a physician three months before his death at Pennsylvania Hospital on Feb. 14, 1915. See Certificate of Death, PA Dept. of Health, File #18549

[104] The early years of Mary Hansen (1874-1952) remain sketchy, but she was born in Denmark and came to the U.S. as a young girl, working as a domestic servant. She met George and bore their son, George Jr., during the years 1892-93. Their daughter Heloise was born in 1904. A dedicated anarchist throughout her life, Hansen wrote reports of local activism, reviews, stories, and poems for movement periodicals. After her partner's death in 1915, she taught at the Ferrer Modern School in Stelton, NJ and

then lived there till her death. Mary is remembered for her warm personality and her love of children.

[105] An extremely severe economic depression began in October 1908. Stock prices dropped by one third, and between the years 1907-08, overall unemployment rose from 1.8% to 8.5%, while in mining, manufacturing, building trades, and transportation it went as high as 16.4%. About 1.2 million people in the Unites States were unemployed in March 1908, the month immediately following the scene Weinberg is describing here. See Robert J. Goldstein, "The Anarchist Scare of 1908;" *American Studies*, vol. XV, #2 (Fall 1974), p. 59.

[106] By "international" Weinberg means that the gathering included various ethnic and language groups.

[107] The intended Italian speaker was the later-famous anarchist Carlo Tresca, who did not appear. In his place Antonio De Bella, the Socialist editor of *Il Proletario* (1123 So. 11th Street) gave the Italian address. Although Weinberg's and de Cleyre's speeches were not understood by the Italians who allegedly rioted, they were arrested while De Bella was never sought by the police. News reports said that Brown would be arrested, but although he waited at his house, only reporters and friends stopped by. See *Philadelphia Record*, Feb. 23, 1908.

[108] The call was made unexpectedly in Italian while George Brown was speaking. Pleas from the speakers for them to stop, in English and Italian, were ignored.

[109] The "Broad Street Riot" took place on Thursday, February 20, 1908, when poor Italian immigrants marched peacefully from the Hall at 747-53 So. 3rd Street, along Catherine Street to Broad, then North toward City Hall. According to the anarchists' account, a van-driver "brutally drove his horses among them" and the Italians defended themselves by knocking the wagon over. The police, mounted on horses and motorized Bicycles, joined in the fray at Broad & Locust (after the march had gone 18 blocks), clubbing heads and arresting people right and left. One Italian fired two shots (apparently at the van-driver), and fourteen were sent to the Moyamensing Prison. The charges were "assault and battery with intent to kill." Police witnesses made exaggerated, implausible statements at the trial, with bullets being stopped by their badges, and bullet-holes in their collars. Only one defendant, Dominick Donelli, was an anarchist, and he received a five-year sentence, allegedly because he was the "most violent." Three others got between one and two years, but

all four were released before the full terms were served. During their imprisonment, the anarchists (mostly by de Cleyre's activism) raised money and supported the families of these poor Italians. Newspaper accounts of the affair painted a far less sympathetic account; one Street Sergeant and three Patrolmen were decorated for their "heroic action" on the day of the riot. See *Annual Report of Henry Clay, Director Department of Public Safety*, Vol. 1 (1909) under "commendations" (Temple University, Urban Archives). For another anarchist statement, see the leaflet "The True History of the Broad St. Riot" (Labadie Collection).

[110] The Colonial Café was located at 514 South 5th Street. Weinberg was arrested there on the night of Feb. 20th, and de Cleyre was collared (with reporters taking pictures outside) at her home (929 Wallace St.) on the following afternoon.

[111] Weinberg may have blurred a few details of the events of 22 years earlier: his bail was reported as $800, and de Cleyre's as $2500. Both were bailed out by comrades who were physicians. There were about 22, not 50, in the lockup, unless the police were giving half the actual figure. Several were released within a few hours.

[112] Henry John Nelson (1874-1930) obtained both a bachelor's degree in Economics (1899), and his law degree (1905) at the University of Pennsylvania. In September 1901 we find him editing the "Labor News" column for the *North American*, and he would represent the famous anarchist Emma Goldman in 1909 when she was blocked from speaking by Philadelphia authorities. See *Evening Bulletin*, Sept. 28, 1909; Alumni Record File, University Archives, U. of Pennsylvania; also Obituary, *Philadelphia Inquirer*, Oct, 2, 1930.

[113] Henry Nathan Wessel (1871-1920) was a partner with the firm Wessel & Aarons, 1112 Chestnut Street, at the time of this trial, having graduated from the University of Pennsylvania Law School in 1891. Weinberg did well by choosing this progressive Nebraska-born attorney, who happened to have begun his career as a lawyer by serving as the assistant to this very same Mayer Sulzberger, before Sulzberger became a judge. This son of German immigrants was orphaned as a boy, but during his career, Wessel was offered a position by William Jennings Bryan's presidential campaign, and he served on the board of the Jewish Hospital, which was founded by Judge Sulzberger's father. He was elected Judge, Court of Common Pleas, in 1916. See the biographical

sketch on Wessel in the *Evening Item*, Sept. 11, 1901; Obituary for Jacob Sulzberger in *Jewish Exponent*, Sept. 17, 1897, and Wessels' alumnus file, Archives of the University of Pennsylvania.

[114] Judge Mayer Sulzberger (1843-1923) was a German-born Jew who arrived in the United States at age six. He was a leading intellectual among the Jews of Philadelphia. See his obituary in *Legal Intelligencer*, May 4, 1923, pp. 369-71. Morris Wolf was the Assistant District Attorney and Ralph Gold was the "special officer" of the 33rd District. See de Cleyre, "The Philadelphia Farce," *Mother Earth*, July 1908.

[115] Actually the Italians were sentenced on Feb. 27, a week after the riot, and the trial for Weinberg and de Cleyre took place months later, on June 18, 1908. The four Italians (see note 18) were sentenced by Judge Robert Von Moschzisker. Judge Von Moschzisker, ironically, was the son of the Austrian "forty-eighter" Franz A. Von Moschzisker (also a distinguished physician and literary scholar), and his home was bombed by unidentified Italian anarchists on December 30, 1918. See Carl Wittke, *Refugees of Revolution: the German Forty-Eighters in America* (1952), and all Philadelphia newspapers from Dec. 31, 1918.

[116] *Boyd's City Directory* for Philadelphia, 1908 reads: Newman Beard, baker, 607 South 7th Street

[117] The witness who swore out the warrant at the arraignment, but failed to appear at the trial, was John Karet of 630 Race Street, who gave extended narrations (from memory) of Weinberg's speech to the magistrate. His quotes were not sensational, but he said that men cheered and stood on chairs while Weinberg spoke. See *Record, Press, Evening Item, North American*, and *Public Ledger,* Feb. 26, 1908.

[118] It should be noted that Judge Sulzberger had the reputation, wrote Voltairine de Cleyre, "of being somewhat more inclined to weigh the rights of citizens as against the attacks of the police than some other judges." Fifteen years later, his obituary article in the *Record* stated that the judge "had a particular aversion to some of the methods of police work, and for a long time he was at open warfare with Director of Public Safety Porter, under the Blankenburg administration, over his attitude toward police witnesses in his court and his leniency to prisoners against whom policemen were the only witnesses." See de Cleyre, "The Philadelphia Farce," *Mother Earth*, July 1908; and the judge's obituary, *Philadelphia Record*, April 21, 1923.

Chapter 8

[119] Actually these events took place during the winter of 1904-05 (see note 5 below).

[120] The 1904 City Directory lists news vender Louis Geventer at 522 South 4th Street.

[121] Apparently Elka Yetta London (July 10, 1886-March 1, 1942) who became Yetta Weinberg, the author's partner. Yetta's death record indicates that she came from the Russian Empire to the United States around 1896. Commonwealth of Pennsylvania, Certificate of Death, file #29193, March 1, 1942. Yetta was twenty-five years younger than Chaim. Her parents' names were Samuel and Anna Rosen London. She is buried at Montefiore Cemetery, Elkins Park, PA.

[122] Joseph J. Cohen, who was to become a key anarchist of the city, had just recently arrived in Philadelphia. In his memoirs, he mentions that "Weinberg was very occupied with... the cooperative house in which a number of young comrades lived. Among them were B. Axler and Y. Katz. They lived very frugally saving every penny they could with the hopes that with their pooled finances they would be able to buy a piece of land and make it into a cooperative farm and enterprise." Cohen, *The Jewish Anarchist Movement in the United States: A Historical Review and Personal Reminiscences.* Philadelphia: Radical Library (1945).

[123] During the winter of 1904-05, Yekaterina (or Catherine) Breshkovskaya (1844-1934) made three lecture stops in the city: November 27 and December 25, 1904, and March 5, 1905. All three events drew ample press coverage, and Weinberg presided at the first. *Babushka* is Russian for "little grandmother." By "parlor radicals," Weinberg may mean the same "lying Social Democrats" as Voltairine de Cleyre resented at the March event. See her letter to Alexander Berkman, Aug. 24, 1906 (Berkman Papers, Amsterdam). Or, he might have meant people from the College Settlement House, such as its leader Anna Davies, who gave Breshkovskaya a "reception and tea" on March 6th along with a group of society women. See reports in *Philadelphia Record, Inquirer, Press,* and *North American,* March 6, 1905.

[124] Chaim Zhitlovsky (1861-1943) is regarded as "one of the most learned and sophisticated Yiddish writers of modern times." His native language was Russian, but he had full command of German and Yiddish. The Russian Social Revolutionary Party recruited him as the one to

accompany Breshkovskaya to the US in 1904, where his speeches were very well received. Zhitlovsky returned permanently to the US in 1909. For a while he was a Social Territorialist (Socialist-Zionist) along with two men who earlier had been very active and well-loved anarchists (Hillel Solotaroff and Moishe Katz). Eventually, he entered the Communist Party. See Melech Epstein, *Profiles of Eleven*. Detroit: Wayne State (1965), pp. 295-322; Steven Cassedy, *To The Other Shore: The Russian Jewish Intellectuals Who Came to America* (Princeton, 1997); Emma Goldman, *Living My Life*, p. 370.

[125] The Yiddish original gives the name Harriman Hospital, which was founded in 1920 in suburban Bucks County. Perhaps the new institution led to either Weinberg's or Marcus Graham's confusion in 1930. Hahnemann Hospital (Broad & Vine Streets), however, was the nearest to any house on Morse Street, and is the same hospital where the wounded Voltairine de Cleyre was taken a few years earlier.

[126] Flora married Caplan and was found by police near La Honda, California and held for questioning when her husband was as yet still at large. *Los Angeles Times,* June 14, 1912, p. 13.

[127] David Caplan was born in Russia and arrived in the United States as a young man. He was expelled after police found "books of a communistic nature" in his student room. In the US, he worked at many trades, including those of streetcar operator and barber. He was implicated in the dynamite bombing of the LA *Times* on Oct. 1, 1910 (which took twenty-one lives), but escaped and went into hiding. He was betrayed by police informer Donald Vose, son of the respected anarchist Gertie Vose, and arrested at Rolling Bay, Washington in February 1915. The trial was held in Los Angeles from Oct. 23 through Dec. 15, 1916, after much energy was devoted to his defense. He was convicted of "voluntary manslaughter" and sentenced to ten years (the maximum). Pauline Jacobsen, writing after his arrest, states that Caplan was "known among his comrades as the most Christ-like Tolstoyan of them all." She refers to his having resided in various cities, but not Philadelphia. See *Organized Labor* (San Francisco) April 17, 1915. Caplan was last spotted in a derelict condition in Europe during the 1940's, but reports of his final years are sketchy and conflict with one another. We surmise that Caplan's actual character was more in keeping with Weinberg's criticisms than with Jacobsen's high praise, written a decade or so after his interlude in Philadelphia.

Chapter 9

[128] Footnote in the 1952 Yiddish edition reads: "In 1903, B. Schlesinger was president of the Cloakmakers' Union. The office was located in a saloon and the saloon-keeper used to come to the aid of the union. He even gave a $300 ring for $75 so that the union would have the money to bring Schlesinger from Chicago to New York."

[129] S. Polakoff, a native of Russia, came to the US as a tailor in 1897. He was not connected with the union from 1917-23, but later was manager of the Baltimore Local. See Levine, *Women's Garment Workers*, page 590.

[130] John A. Dyche (1867-1938) was born in Russia, then was active in the Socialist and labor movement in England before coming to New York in 1901 as a shirtmaker. General Secretary and Treasurer of the International Ladies' Garment Workers Union 1904-1914. He later went into business. See Levine, page 583.

[131] Weinberg seems to refer here to the same Sam Shore as he mentions again in chapter 10, and who is described by Levine as "native of Russia; for a number of years manager of White Goods Workers' Union; later connected with the International Union Bank." See Levine, page 592

[132] Saul Yanovsky (1872-1959) was, in the late 1880's, a member of the first Jewish anarchist group in the US, called Pioneers of Freedom. In 1889 he moved to London to edit *Der Arbeter Fraynd*. He was a very able speaker and would share platforms with the leading figures in the movement. After five years in the UK he returned to New York. He was editor of the *Fraye Arbeter Shtime*, the leading Yiddish anarchist paper, from 1899-1919 and remained a prominent figure into the 1930's.

[133] There was a politically and religiously conservative *Yiddishes Tageblatt* in New York at that time, but also a *Jewish Daily News* founded 1901 at Philadelphia, with its text in Yiddish, but neither seems to be the paper referred to here.

[134] Arthur Bookman (1877-1973) graduated Colombia College in 1897 and Columbia School of Medicine in 1901. He maintained a practice in Manhattan throughout his career. See Alumni Records, Columbia University Archives.

[135] Hillel Solotaroff (1865-1921) was a very active, respected anarchist and journalist in addition to his distinguished career in Medicine on New

York's Lower East Side. His 3-volume *Geklibene Shriften* (Collected Works) was published in 1924.

[136] *Gemore* tune: a tune that would accompany the words, as one studied a part of the Talmud.

[137] Dr. Fred Houdlett Albee (1876-1945) was one of the world's leading orthopedic surgeons. He once explained his bone-grafting technique by saying, "all I have done is apply the principles of tree-grafting and cabinetmaking to my method." See obituary, *New York Times*, Feb. 16, 1945

[138] Abe Kaplan, 19 years old, was shot and killed instantly by 39-year old Tony Cartese during a street battle involving about 100 people at the corner of Seventh and Spruce Streets. He fell dead on the steps of the First Presbyterian Church (NE corner). The funeral drew a crowd estimated at 15,000. See *Press, Record*, and *Inquirer*, Oct. 24; *Press*, Oct. 27, 1913. Today, Kaplan's tombstone at Mount Lebanon Cemetery in Darby, PA reads "Killed in General Strike October 23, 1913."

[139] Max Amdur (sometimes spelled Emdur) is described by Levine as a native of Russia who was a cloakmakers' union leader in Philadelphia from 1907. He was a Vice President of the International at the time of the 1913 strike. See Levine, page 581.

[140] This meeting took place on Wednesday, September 24, 1913. The news reports stated that "over 3,500 men and women" packed the Academy of Music. "A touch of the dramatic was added to the scene when Amdur slowly tore up the communication from the manufacturers, and the strikers, as the pieces fluttered to the floor, jumped to their feet and applauded continuously for several minutes." Another speaker was B. Vladek, who is mentioned again in chapter 18. It was noted that Weinberg, "a veteran in the strikers' ranks," had to be assisted to the speakers' platform. On the previous night, seven male strikers were arrested for allegedly "laying siege to" the home of an employer named Morris Sleppin in West Philadelphia, and in two cases, they were also charged with carrying revolvers. See *Record* and *Public Ledger*, Sept. 25, 1913.

Chapter 10

[141] These are Jacob L. Joffe (b. 1871) and Julius Moscowitz, who was arrested in connection to the Yom Kippur Ball affair in 1891, described in Chapter 4. A *khevre-kadishe* is a burial society.

[142] About Louis Miller, see Chapter 3, note 11.

[143] The strike took place during the summer of 1890.

[144] William Edlin, (1878-1947) wrote a Yiddish book about operas in 1907.

[145] By committeeman, Weinberg means what would later be called a shop steward (tr.) He is describing union meetings with guest speakers.

Chapter 11

[146]Lithuanian-born Morris Winchevsky (1856-1932) began writing at age seventeen, under his original name, Lippe Benzion Novakhovitz. From there he acquired Socialism in Russia and then Germany, from which he was deported for his politics in 1878. Arriving in London's East End, He sought out Johann Most and contributed to *Freiheit*; also knew Peter Lavrov. Taking on the name Winchevsky in the 1880's, when he wrote for both anarchist and socialist papers in English and Yiddish, becoming one of the four legendary "sweatshop poets," and a writer of international reputation. By the time he moved to the United Satates in 1894, he had become exclusively socialist in his politics while remaining an independent thinker and on good terms with anarchists. From the 1920's, however, he was aligned with the Communist Party. See Melech Epstein, *Profiles of Eleven* (1965), pp. 13-48.

[147] Yitskhak-Isaac Halevi Hurvitsh, or I. A. Gurvitch, but usually spelled Isaac A. Hourwich (1860-1924), a statistician and lawyer, lectured at both the University of Chicago and George Washington University. He immigrated to the United States from Russia in the early 1890's, having been exiled to Siberia before that. Between 1888 and 1922, Hourwich wrote several books on Russian law and economy, immigration, banking, mining industry statistics, and labor. He also had a successful career as a journalist, in both Russian and Yiddish. See Levine, *The Women's Garment Workers*, p. 586, and Steven Cassedy, *To The Other Shore* (Princeton, 1997), p. 10.

Chapter 12

[148] Meyer London (1871-1927) was born in Russia and came to New York's Lower East Side at age 20. His father, Ephraim London, briefly published the anarchist paper *Morgenstern*, but Meyer was a socialist throughout his career. He was a lawyer who often defended poor Jews for free, and was an invaluable ally to labor. He was elected to the US House of Representatives in 1914 and 1916, but lost narrowly in 1918. He took bold stands against the mistreatment of conscientious objectors and the suppression of radicalism, and when he was killed by a taxi, he was mourned as an idealist of the highest order in hundreds of obituaries. See Melech Epstein, *Profiles of Eleven*, Detroit: Wayne State (1965), pp. 161-187.

[149] The Industrial Workers of the World (IWW), founded in 1905, has drawn much scrutiny from historians, folklorists, and of course the authorities, both because of its militantly syndicalist philosophy and for the legendary determination of its members during strikes, anti-war campaigns, and Free Speech fights. Its Preamble begins, "The working class and the employing class have nothing in common," and its members are called "the Wobblies." There were thirty-seven IWW locals in Philadelphia from 1906-1916; among them was bakery workers' Local 405, which existed from 1912 and held a strike in May, 1917. IWW still exists, and it always has had many anarchist members. For the present reference, see William Stambaugh, *The Industrial Workers of the World in Pennsylvania* (Master's Thesis) Pennsylvania State University at Harrisburg, (1998), pages 111-119.

[150] The Exodus from Egypt was evidently one of Weinberg's popular lecture titles. The Jewish audience would recognize that the topic was redemption from slavery.

[151] He means the Director of Public Safety, whose office controlled the Police Department, the Fire Department, and all the building inspectors. During WWI, they were George D. Porter (1911-16), then William H. Wilson (1916-19). Usually called the Director, they were appointed by the mayor of Philadelphia. The famous Arch Street Theatre stood at 6th & Arch Streets.

Chapter 13

[152] Isidore Prenner, (or Brenner) has appeared in Chapters 3 and 4, with biographical notes. He had parted paths with the anarchists during the fall of 1892.

[153] Nathan Birnbaum (1864-1937) of Vienna actually coined the term *Zionism,* but left the movement in 1898 to promote Diaspora Nationalism, and then extreme religious orthodoxy before the start of World War I. He toured the United States in early 1908. See *Encyclopaedia Judaica*, Vol. 4, columns 1039-42.

[154] Birnbaum's Philadelphia lecture took place (in German) on the evening of February 18, 1908, two days before the meeting related to the "Broad Street Riot" (see Chapter 7), and in the same venue (New Auditorium Hall on South 3rd Street). Prenner was on the event's committee. See "Dr. Nathan Birnbaum Here," *Jewish Exponent*, Feb. 21, 1908.

[155] Aside from their radical lives, Max Staller was a surgeon and a specialist in tuberculosis, while Leo N. Gartman was a urologist, specializing in venereal diseases.   Both these physicians were distinguished in the profession.

Chapter 14

[156] The expulsion began in March 28, 1891 and reached its peak during the following winter. At least 30,000 Jews were driven out of the city, while some 5,000 remained. See *Encyclopaedia Judaica*, Vol. 12, p. 364.

[157] President Marie Francois Sadi Carnot was stabbed to death by the Italian anarchist Sante Caserio at Lyon on June 24, 1894.

[158] We know the inspirational quality of David Edelstadt's songs from ample testimony, including that of Emma Goldman, who described him as "a spiritual petrel whose songs of revolt were beloved by every Yiddish-speaking radical." See Goldman, *Living My Life* (1931) p. 55.

[159] The mourner's *Kaddish* is recited for eleven months after the death of a parent, and thereafter on the anniversary of the death. This tradition is so important that a first or an only son is sometimes called a *Kaddish*, because his birth implies that the parents have someone who will eventually recite the prayer in their memory.

[160] Weinberg also mentions "Sholem's Cafeteria" at the beginning of Chapter 11.

Chater 15

[161] Harry Gordon (1866-1941) and his wife Lydia Landau Gordon were both devoted, Russian-Jewish anarchists. They met in Chicago, shortly after the incident described here. Harry saw other women aside from Lydia, but they remained together permanently. It is not clear to whom Weinberg refers as Gordon's girlfriend, but Emma Goldman remembers an earlier "Mrs. Gordon" in Pittsburgh, 1897, as "a simple, tender-hearted woman" who "always went out of her way" to make Goldman comfortable at their home when she visited the city. See Goldman, *Living My Life* (1931), p. 198; also Avrich, *Anarchist Voices* (1999) pp. 273-281.

[162] Of course he means the Ku Klux Klan: Weinberg is making the reference only a few years after the revival of the organization began around 1925.

[163] The Mohegan Colony was founded by anarchists at Lake Mohegan, NY in 1923. Harry Gordon and his family were among its original members. See Avrich, *Anarchist Voices*, p. 195.

[164] Lev Solomon Moiseev, who signed his name as M. Leontieff, was born in 1873 and edited *Di Fraye Gezelshaft* (The Free Society), a very fine anarchist journal, from 1895-1900 in New York. As an engineer he supervised the construction of both the Williamsburg and Manhattan Bridges, which cross the city's East River. He also consulted for the George Washington Bridge, which bears a plaque in his honor. See Avrich, *Anarchist Portraits* (Princeton, 1988), pp. 186-87, 292 note 38.

[165] That is to say, how they suffered through the difficulties of the early years (tr).

[166] The Russian chemist Dmitri Ivanovich Mendeleev (1834-1907) is best remembered for having invented the periodic table of the elements.

[167] "Jewish World" (tr.)

[168] We should stop to examine the arithmetic of age between Yetta (born July 10, 1886) and Chaim (born c.1860). If, in 1926, they had been living together for 27 years, then the cohabitation began in 1899, when Yetta was 13 years old. That year would also coincide with the birth of Chaim's unexplained son, mentioned in passing in Chapter 15. In Chapter 16, however, he writes that in 1911 when he settled in Willow Grove and Yetta was 25, he "became better acquainted with Comrade

Yetta London." Another mention of Yetta is in 1905 (she was 19), when
the cooperative house was started on Morse Street (see Chapter 8).

Chapter 16

[169] Max N. Maisel (1872-1959), a Jewish anarchist, ran a radical
bookstore on the Lower East Side in New York City for decades. He
was also distributed anarchist periodicals and published many works,
including authors like Kropotkin, Thoreau, Oscar Wilde, and John
Dyche, who Weinberg mentions in Chapter 9. Abe Isaak started working
at Maisel's some time after 1901. See Avrich, *Anarchist Voices,* page 25;
page 483, note 72.

[170] The streetcar strike of 1910 was an extremely bitter one, beginning
with a walkout on February 19. Weinberg arrived in California before
April 24. See de Cleyre, "The Philadelphia Strike," *Mother Earth*, March
1910, pp. 7-10; also, Letter, De Cleyre to Livshis, April 24, 1910,
Labadie Collection.

[171] This was called the Aurora Colony, located at Lincoln, California.
See Avrich, *Anarchist Voices*, pp. 23-28.

[172] Abe Isaak (1856-1937) remained on the farm until his death.

[173] Voltairine de Cleyre saw Weinberg in Chicago during this tour. In a
private letter, she states, "Weinberg is here now; he sold his land in
California; says it is impossible to live there. Same old story: Sarah had
to be 'Mrs. Weinberg' because 'the surrounding farmers would burn our
houses down,' etc." See de Cleyre to Mary Hansen, June 3, 1911; Joseph
Ishill Collection, Houghton Library, Harvard University.

[174] *Note from the 1952 Yiddish edition:* "The reader should remember
here that Comrade Weinberg imparted his recollections to me in the year
1930, when I spent several weeks at his home, and that the recollections
related above correctly describe the last cooperative experiment, in
which he had taken part up to that time. In fact, however, it wasn't the
final cooperative experiment in which Comrade Weinberg participated.

"Some years later, after 1930, when the Sunrise Cooperative Colony
was founded, Comrade Weinberg asked my opinion about his plan to
join the new colony. I was in California at that time, where I was editing
the anarchist journal *Man!* (1933-1940), a journal of which Comrade
Weinberg was a faithful reader. In my reply, I expressed a doubt whether
the experiment was not too colossal, right from the start, which would
require overly large yearly sums to support. I ended my answer with the

advice that he had given me years before, when I had been eager to know his opinion about my cooperative plans for the Radical Library. "You have, of course, already heard about my many disappointments," Comrade Weinberg said to me then, "Now go and carry out your plans – disregarding that!"

"And, as everyone knows, Comrade Weinberg and his life companion Yetta London joined the Sunrise Colony. After being there for almost two years, they withdrew from it, disenchanted, and returned to their farm in Willow Grove. There they both lived to the end of his life, in 1939. A few years later, Yetta Weinberg also died. – Marcus Graham"

Note further that the Sunrise Cooperative Colony was started at Alicia, Michigan, in 1933, and led by Weinberg's old Philadelphia comrade Joseph J. Cohen. See "Weinberg at Sunrise" in this volume, for Cohen's remarks.

Chapter 17

[175] Leonard Dalton Abbott (1878-1953) was an editor for *Current Literature*, a socialist and freethinker who converted from socialism to anarchism around 1910. He was very widely respected and liked, and frequently contributed to the major anarchist journals of the day. See Avrich, *Anarchist Voices*, p. 479, note 34.

[176] De Cleyre's grave is a few yards from those of the Haymarket martyrs, Emma Goldman, and many others, in Waldheim, originally the German section of Chicago's Forest Lawn Cemetery.

[177] Ben L. Reitman (1879-1942) was arrested at Moose Hall in Cleveland on December 12, 1916. The trial opened on January 10th before Judge Dan Cull. He was sentenced to six months in prison, but released on bail pending an appeal. See Roger A. Bruns, *The Damndest Radical* (1987), pp. 180-188.

[178] News of the revolution spread in the last week of February, 1917, and the Czar abdicated on March 2.

[179] V. M. Eikhenbaum (1882-1945), known as Volin, was indeed editor of *Golos Truda* (Voice of Labor), and later of *Nabat* (Tocsin). In 1915, Volin was living in France, and he learned that the government intended to imprison him for his anti-war activism. With the help of French comrades he sailed from Bordeaux to New York. Returning to Russia, he

was involved in the Anarchist force led by Nestor Makhno, against both the Bolshevik and Tzarist forces. The cremated remains of both are in Pere Lachaise Cemetery, Paris. See Volin, *The Unknown Revolution 1917-1921*; Forward by Rudolf Rocker (New York: Free Life Eds., 1974), p. 11.

[180] V. S. (Bill) Shatoff came from Russia to the U.S. in 1907. During his time in the states, he was an active IWW unionist and wandering jack-of-all-trades, including, for a while, a longshoreman in Philadelphia. Shatoff was a respected early member of the Ferrer Modern School. He returned to Russia in 1917, becoming one of the four anarchist members of Military Revolutionary Committee, which engineered the seizure of power under Trotsky's leadership in October of that year. He rose to high rank and distinction as a Bolshevik leader, but never completely shunned his old anarchist friends. He was finally arrested and shot during the purges of 1937-38. See Avrich, *The Modern School Movement* (1980), pp. 120, 332-34.

Chapter 18

[181] William Shulman (c. 1881-Oct. 14, 1935) arrived in the US from his native Russia around 1903 and worked first as a pants maker, later in a grocery store. Shulman was a passionate, lifetime anarchist and atheist, as well as a member of the Radical Library group in Philadelphia. His home life did not harmonize with his beliefs. When he died, his wishes for cremation without religious ceremony were overruled by his family. See the obituary in *Man!*, November & December issues, 1935. Shulman's tombstone stands in the Workmen's Circle B Section of Montefiore Cemetery.

[182] Sam Goldenberg, originally a tailor by trade, was indeed an "Arbeter Fraynter." He got his start on the stage at the group's Workers' Friend Club on Jubilee Street, London, which opened in 1906, and later became a star of the international Yiddish theater. See Fishman, *East End Jewish Radicals*, pp. 262-65.

[183] Having a "matchless voice of incomparable mellowness, depth, and power," Sophie Braslau (1892-1935) was the only child of the physician Abel Braslau (1861-1925) and his wife Alexandra Goodelman Braslau, two very cultured Ukranian-born anarchists of New York City. In a career that lasted 21 years, Sophie sang and spoke fluently in seven

languages. When Weinberg's party took place, she was just beginning to take on starring roles at the New York Metropolitan Opera. Her most celebrated song was the "Spring Song of the Robin Woman," which she performed as the Indian maiden in C. W. Cadman's *Shanewis*. Along the way she drew high acclaim in concert tours of the U.S. and Europe, and by 1930, when Weinberg wrote this recollection, she had become famous by singing live on the newly-established CBS Radio and through commercial recordings. Sophie died of lung cancer. See Edward Hagelin Pearson, "Sophie Braslau," *The Record Collector,* March, 1996; also Emma Goldman, *Living My Life, pp. 369-70.*

Chapter 19

[184] Anarchists in Weinberg's day often held views that overlapped with other philosophies, or else avoided adding any adjectives (such as communist, individualist, or revolutionary) onto their anarchism. In some cases they used alternative terms in place of anarchism (e.g. libertarian socialism).

[185] Although U.S. President Woodrow Wilson was involved in its creation, the United States never joined the League of Nations, which was founded in 1920 to prevent another world war.

[186] The book (published in English) is Joseph J. Cohen, *In Quest Of Heaven: The Story of the Sunrise Cooperative Farm Community.* Sunrise History Publishing Committee: New York (1957). The passage appears on pages 65-67. In this Cold War-era book, where many names are reduced to the person's initials, Weinberg appears in various places as "Comrade H. W.," as Hyman Weinberg, and in the present passage as "Hayim." We have brought it back to the standard spelling, Chaim, to avoid confusion.

[187] See letter, de Cleyre to Cohen, dated Thurs. a.m. April 22 [1909], in Cohen Papers, Bund Archives, YIVO.

[188] See Chapter 8 for Weinberg's account of the scandal.

Appendix A

[189] Abraham Frumkin, *In friling fun Yidishn sotsializm: zikhroynes fun a zhurnalist* [In *The Spring of Jewish Socialism: Memoirs of a Journalist*] New York: Frumkin Jubilee Committee, 1940.

[190] Baron and Kaplan are described by Weinberg in Chapter 6.

[191] This was de Cleyre's first visit to Britain, arriving June 19, leaving in late October, 1897. See Avrich, *An American Anarchist*, pp. 108-120.

[192] This is a well-known saying from Talmud, Megillah (tr.).

Appendix C

[193] Little biographical information is available for Samuel Polinow, but most of what we have comes in the form of unfavorable remarks. Remembered by contemporary anarchists as "a bit of a screwball –an anarcho-moron" who drank excessively, Polinow was a regular contributor of essays and short fiction to the anarchist periodicals *Road to Freedom* and *Man!* between 1926 and 1940. The remainder of this piece has been left out to spare the reader some clumsy and corny flourishes; even the portion presented here required editing for clarity. See Avrich, *Anarchist Voices*, pp 420, 433. The name Max Polinoff, perhaps a brother of Samuel's, appears as the informant on Weinberg's certificate of death in 1939 (see Chapter 1, note 1). We seem to find this man in 1930, spelled Polinofsky, living at 2930 N Arizona Street in Philadelphia. This cigar factory worker and his wife Lena were 36, having come from Russia in 1904 and 1913 respectively. Their children Ruth, George, and Riba were 8, 6, and 4 years old. They were native Yiddish speakers who also spoke English. (*1930 Federal Population Census*, reel T626-3113, 13A, e.d. 690; 0261, lines 46-50). It is peculiar that although Samuel Polinow was a very prominent contributor to *Man!*, editor Marcus Graham omitted to describe him in his 1974 anthology of the paper.

[194] Yasnaya Polyana was the home of the great Russian intellectual Leo Tolstoy, who was an anarchist in his later years. Many anarchists and other reformers visited him there.

[195] This essay appeared during the final weeks of the Spanish Civil War, which was tragic and disappointing on an epic scale for the anarchist movement. Earlier in the war, anarchist collectives and militia controlled about one-third of Spain.

Appendix D

[196] This translates the article as it was excerpted in the Yiddish edition of this book, with the deletions (...) left in place. The date of the piece, evidently written about ten years after Weinberg's death, was not given.

[197] Hebrew for: words that come from the heart. The whole saying is "Words that come from the heart, enter into the heart" (tr.).

[198] Perhaps he is referring here to paying wages in scrip (tr.).

[199] Malamut probably means the Aurora Colony in California (1911), and Sunrise Colony at Alicia, Michigan (begun in 1933). As far as we know, Weinberg was never involved in the colony at Stelton, near New Brunswick, New Jersey, which was founded in 1915.

Appendix E

[200] Leon Kobrin (1872-1946), the Yiddish novelist and playwright, arrived in the United States in 1892. He wrote about 30 plays, and also translated and sometimes adapted for the Yiddish stage, works by Shakespeare, Tolstoy, Chekhov, Maupassant, and Zola. See *Encyclopaedia Judaica*, Vol. 10, columns 1124-25.

[201] This is translated from Weinberg's 1952 book, not from the *Morgn Freiheit*.

[202] Chaim N. Bialik (1873-1934), a poet, prose writer, and publisher, was born in Lithuania and had a celebrated career that found him in Odessa, Berlin, and finally Tel Aviv, where he has been called the National Poet of Israel since before the time of his death.

[203] An allusion to the Biblical Jacob, who made an agreement to work for Laban for seven years in order to marry his daughter Rachel. Perhaps suspecting that Laban would try to substitute another girl, Jacob described Rachel in very specific terms (tr).

[204] This was apparently Leo Hartmann, sometimes called Somoff, the Russian-Bohemian revolutionary who relocated, with a large reward on his head by the Tzar, to New York, Canada, and London starting in 1881, finally settling in New York in 1889. He spoke German as well. That year he was a scheduled speaker for the Bastille-fest held by the city's German and Bohemian anarchist groups. One source has him renouncing Nihilism in 1886. See *Freiheit,* May 25, 1889; George E. McDonald, *Fifty Years of Freethought: The Story of the Truth Seeker* (New York 1929), p. 395.

[205] Henry Clay Frick (1849-1919), an especially warlike enemy of organized labor, ran the vast facility of the Carnegie Steel Company at Homestead, Pennsylvania. Taking advantage of the financial panic of 1873, Frick expanded his holdings in the steel industry by buying up bankrupt companies, and merged with Carnegie in 1889. In 1892 he determined to destroy the Amalgamated Association of Iron and Steel Workers. Alexander Berkman, a 21-year-old Russian-Jewish anarchist, attempted to kill Frick at the coal baron's office on July 23, 1892. Both men pursued their respective causes for the rest of their lives: Berkman served 14 years, then co-edited the leading anarchist communist paper *Mother Earth* for 10 years and wrote the major classics *Prison Memoirs of an Anarchist* and *The Bolshevik Myth*. Henry Frick became one of the richest U.S. citizens of all time.

Index